punch!CAD

I0020745

ViaCAD EXERCISES

200 PRACTICE DRAWINGS

SACHIDANAND JHA

2D / 3D

cadin360°
Learning Tutorials

©Copyright 2019 CADIN360, All rights reserved

Dear Reader,

Thank you for choosing **ViaCAD EXERCISES** book. This book is part of a family of premium-quality CADIN360 books, all of which are written by Outstanding author who combine practical experience with a gift for teaching.

CADIN360 was founded in 2016. More than 3 years later, we're still committed to producing consistently exceptional books. With each of our titles, we're working hard to set a new standard for the industry. From the paper we print on, to the authors we work with, our goal is to bring you the best books available.

I hope you see all that reflected in these pages. I'd be very interested to hear your comments and get your feedback on how we're doing. Feel free to let me know what you think about this or any other CADin360 book by sending me an email at contactus@cadin360.com.

If you think you've found a technical error in this book, please visit https://cadin360.com/contact-us/.
Customer feedback is critical to our efforts at CADIN360.

Best regards,

Sachidanand Jha
Founder & CEO, CADIN360

ViaCAD EXERCISES

Published by
CADIN360
cadin360.com

Copyright © 2019 by CADIN360, All rights reserved.

This book is copyrighted and the CADIN360 reserves all rights.
No part of this publication may be reproduced, stored in a retrieval system or transmitted, transcribed, stored in retrieval system or translated into any language, in any form or by any means, electronic, mechanical, photocopying, recording, scanning or otherwise, without the prior written permission of the publisher & Author.

Limit of Liability/Disclaimer of Warranty:

The publisher and the author make no representations or warranties with respect to the accuracy or completeness of the contents of this work and specifically disclaim all warranties, including without limitation warranties of fitness for a particular purpose. No warranty may be created or extended by sales or promotional materials. The advice and strategies contained herein may not be suitable for every situation. This work is sold with the understanding that the publisher is not engaged in rendering legal, accounting, or other professional services. If professional assistance is required, the services of a competent professional person should be sought. Neither the publisher nor the author shall be liable for damages arising herefrom. The fact that an organization or Web site is referred to in this work as a citation and/or a potential source of further information does not mean that the author or the publisher endorses the information the organization or Web site may provide or recommendations it may make. Further, readers should be aware that Internet Web sites listed in this work may have changed or disappeared between when this work was written and when it is read.

Examination Copies

Books received as examination copies in any form such as paperback and eBook are for review only and may not be made available for the use of the student. These files may not be transferred to any other party. Resale of examination copies is prohibited

Electronic Files

The electronic file/eBook in any form of this book is licensed to the original user only and may not be transferred to any other party.

Disclaimer:

All trademarks and registered trademarks appearing in this book are the property of their respective owners.

Preface

ViaCAD EXERCISES

❖ This book contain 200 CAD practice exercises and drawings.

❖ This book does not provide step by step tutorial to design 3D models.

❖ S.I Units is used.

❖ Predominantly used Third Angle Projection.

❖ This book is for **ViaCAD** and Other Feature-Based Modeling Software such as Inventor, Catia, SolidWorks, NX, Solid Edge, AutoCAD, PTC Creo etc.

❖ It is intended to provide Drafters, Designers and Engineers with enough CAD exercises for practice on **ViaCAD**.

❖ It includes almost all types of exercises that are necessary to provide, clear, concise and systematic information required on industrial machine part drawings.

❖ Third Angle Projection is intentionally used to familiarize Drafters, Designers and Engineers in Third Angle Projection to meet the expectation of world wide Engineering drawing print.

❖ Clear and well drafted drawing help easy understanding of the design.

❖ This book is for Beginner, Intermediate and Advance CAD users.

❖ These exercises are from Basics to Advance level.

❖ Each exercises can be assigned and designed separately.

❖ No Exercise is a prerequisite for another. All dimensions are in mm.

❖ Note: Assume any missing dimensions.

©Copyright 2019 CADIN360, All rights reserved

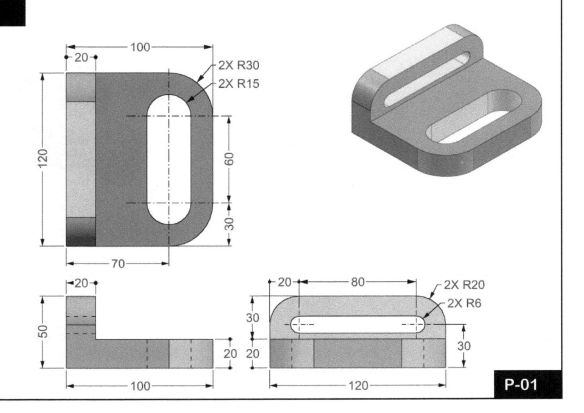

EX-01

Ø80

3 HOLES Ø10
DRILLED THROUGH

R16

28

28 A

A

28

10

5

SECTION A-A

EX-02

100

20

2X R30
2X R15

120

60

30

70

20

50

100

20

20

20

80

30

2X R20
2X R6

30

120

P-01

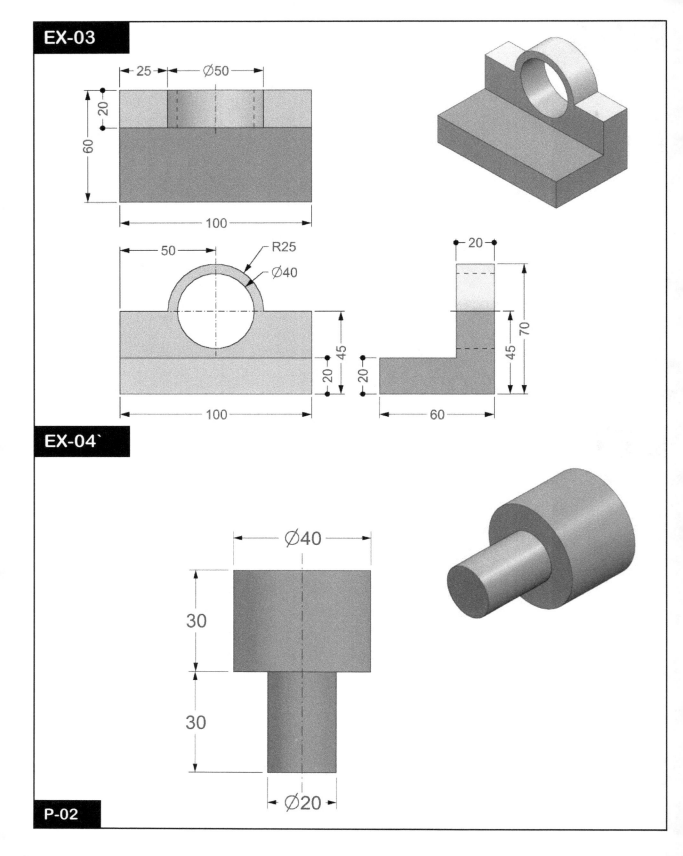

EX-03

25 Ø50

20

60

100

50 R25
Ø40

45
20 20

100

20

70
45

60

EX-04`

Ø40

30

30

Ø20

P-02

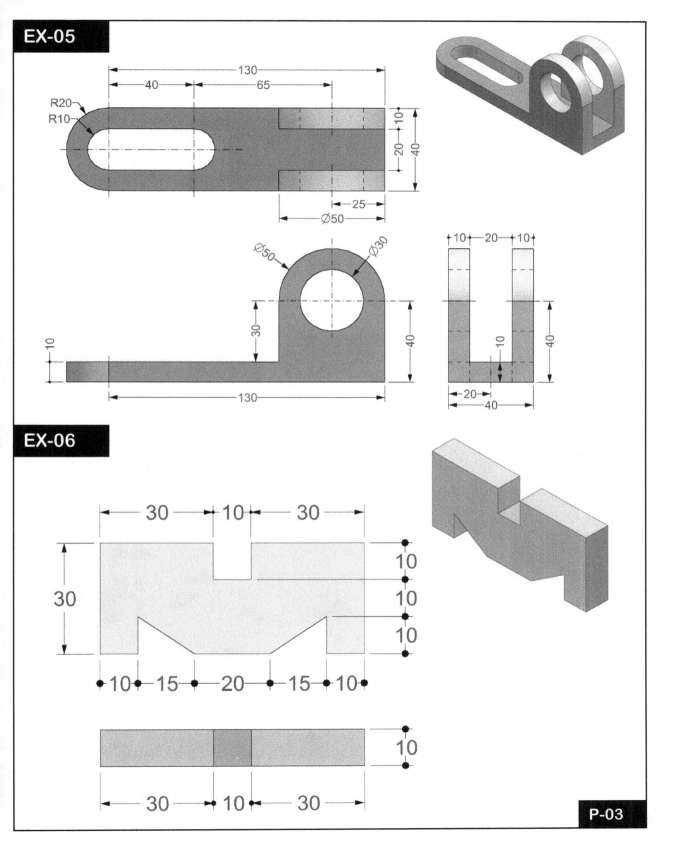

EX-05

EX-06

P-03

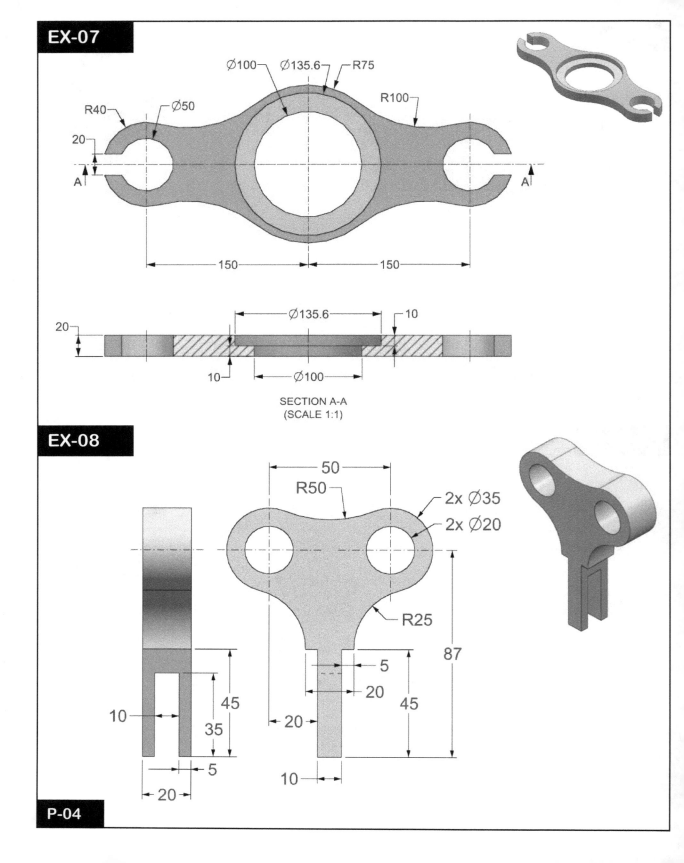

EX-07

Ø100 Ø135.6 R75
R40 Ø50 R100
20
A
150 150

20
Ø135.6 10
10 Ø100

SECTION A-A
(SCALE 1:1)

EX-08

50
R50
2x Ø35
2x Ø20
R25
87
5
20
45
10
45
35
20
5
20
10

P-04

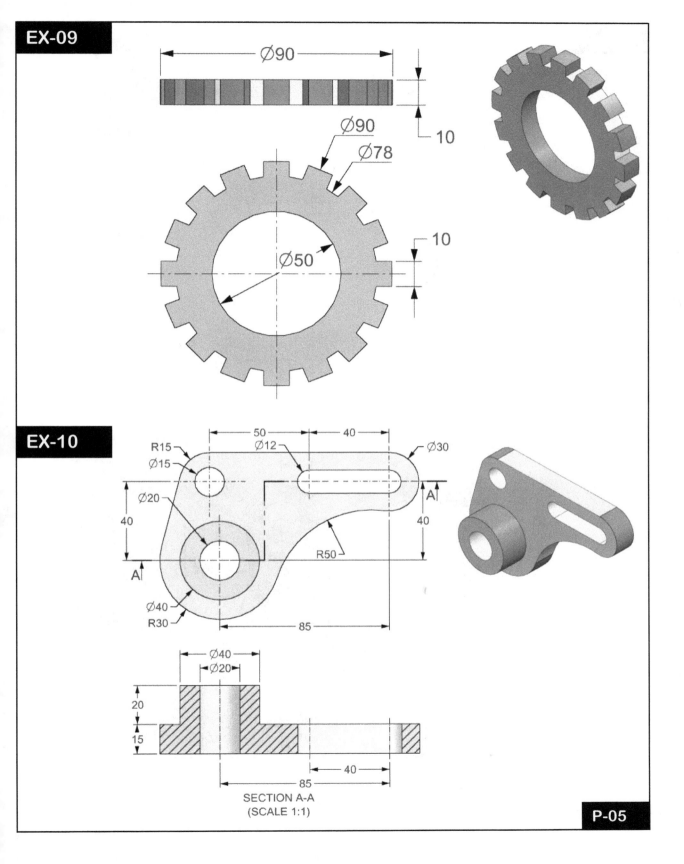

EX-09

⌀90

10

⌀90
⌀78
⌀50

10

EX-10

50
40

R15
⌀15
⌀12
⌀30

⌀20

A

40

40

R50

A

R30
⌀40

85

⌀40
⌀20

20

15

40

85

SECTION A-A
(SCALE 1:1)

P-05

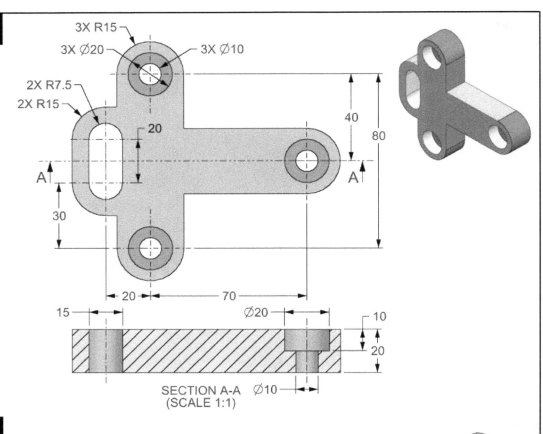

3X R15
3X Ø20
3X Ø10
2X R7.5
2X R15
20
40
80
A
30
20
70
15
Ø20
10
20
SECTION A-A
(SCALE 1:1)
Ø10

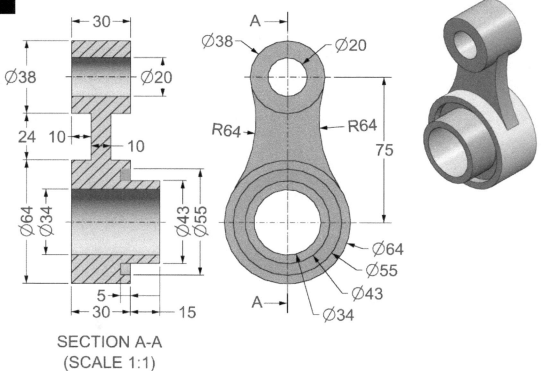

30
Ø38
Ø20
24 10
10
Ø64
Ø34
Ø43
Ø55
5
30
15
A
Ø38
Ø20
R64
R64
75
Ø64
Ø55
Ø43
Ø34
A

SECTION A-A
(SCALE 1:1)

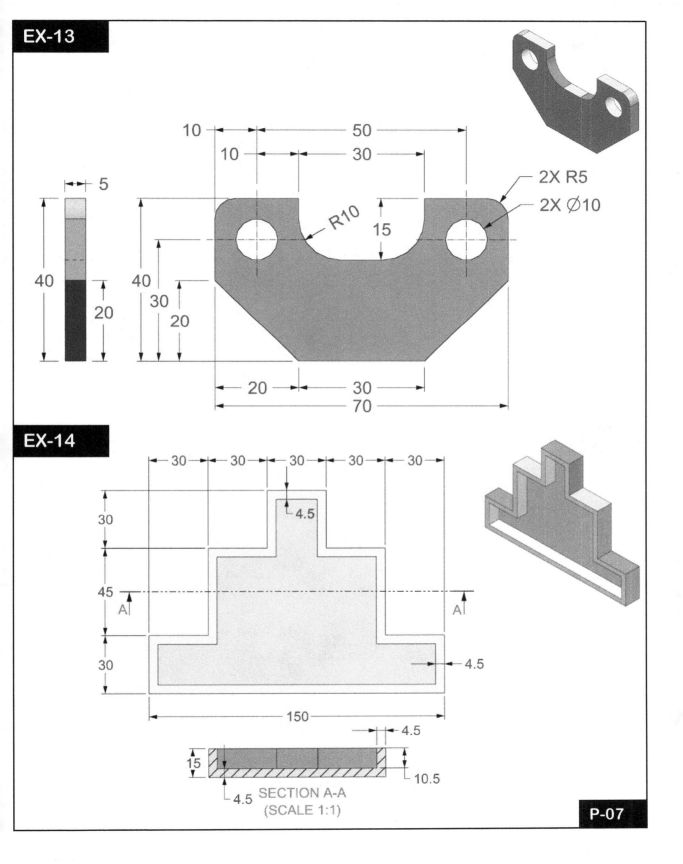

EX-13

10 · 50
10 · 30
5
R10
15
2X R5
2X Ø10
40 · 20
40 · 30 · 20
20 · 30
70

EX-14

30 · 30 · 30 · 30 · 30
30
4.5
45
A · A
30
150
4.5

15 · 4.5 · 10.5 · 4.5
SECTION A-A
(SCALE 1:1)

P-07

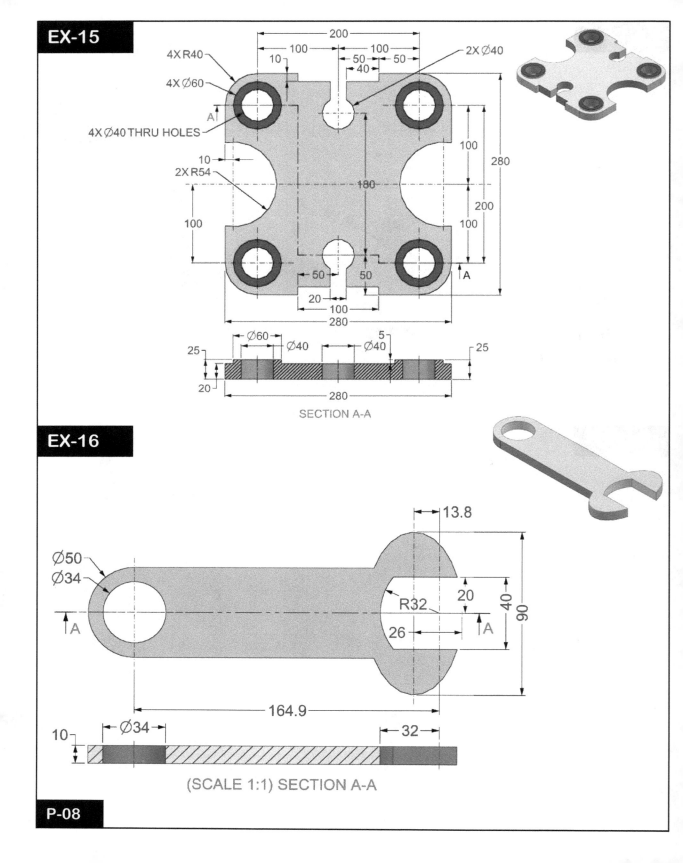

EX-15

4X R40
4X Ø60
4X Ø40 THRU HOLES
2X Ø40
2X R54

200
100
100
10
50
50
40
10
100
280
180
200
100
100
100
50
50
20
100
280

SECTION A-A

Ø60
Ø40
Ø40
5
25
25
25
20
280

EX-16

Ø50
Ø34
13.8
R32
20
40
90
26
164.9
A

(SCALE 1:1) SECTION A-A

Ø34
32
10

P-08

EX-17

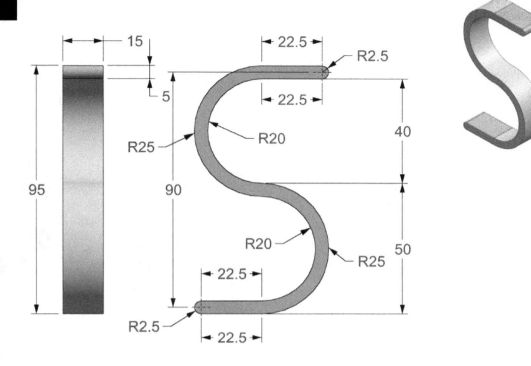

15

22.5

R2.5

5

22.5

R25

R20

40

95

90

R20

50

R25

22.5

R2.5

22.5

22.5

EX-18

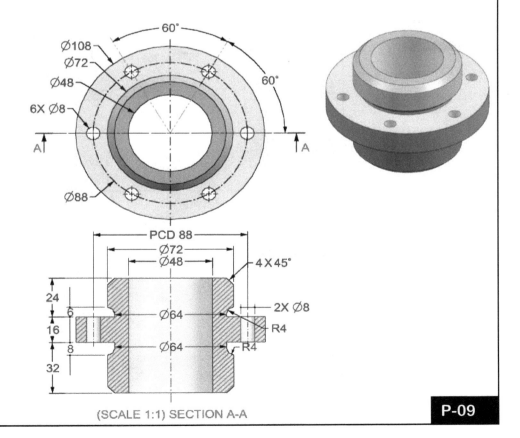

60°

Ø108

Ø72

Ø48

60°

6X Ø8

A ─── A

Ø88

PCD 88

Ø72

Ø48

4 X 45°

24

6

Ø64

2X Ø8

16

R4

8

Ø64

R4

32

(SCALE 1:1) SECTION A-A

P-09

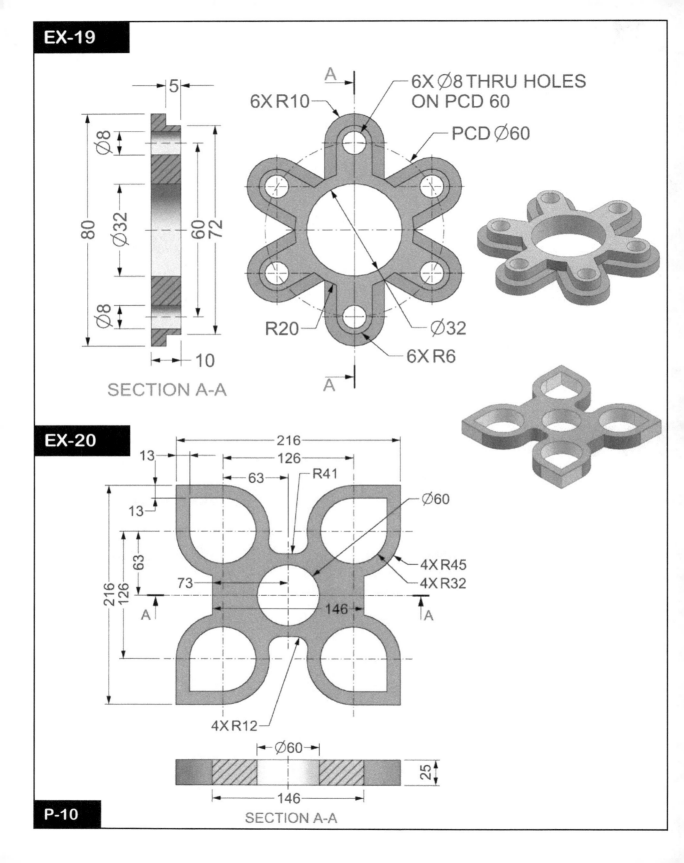

EX-19

5

⌀8

80

⌀32

60

72

⌀8

10

SECTION A-A

A

6X R10

6X ⌀8 THRU HOLES
ON PCD 60

PCD ⌀60

R20

⌀32

6X R6

A

EX-20

216

13

126

63

R41

13

⌀60

63

216

126

73

4X R45

4X R32

146

A

A

4X R12

⌀60

25

146

SECTION A-A

P-10

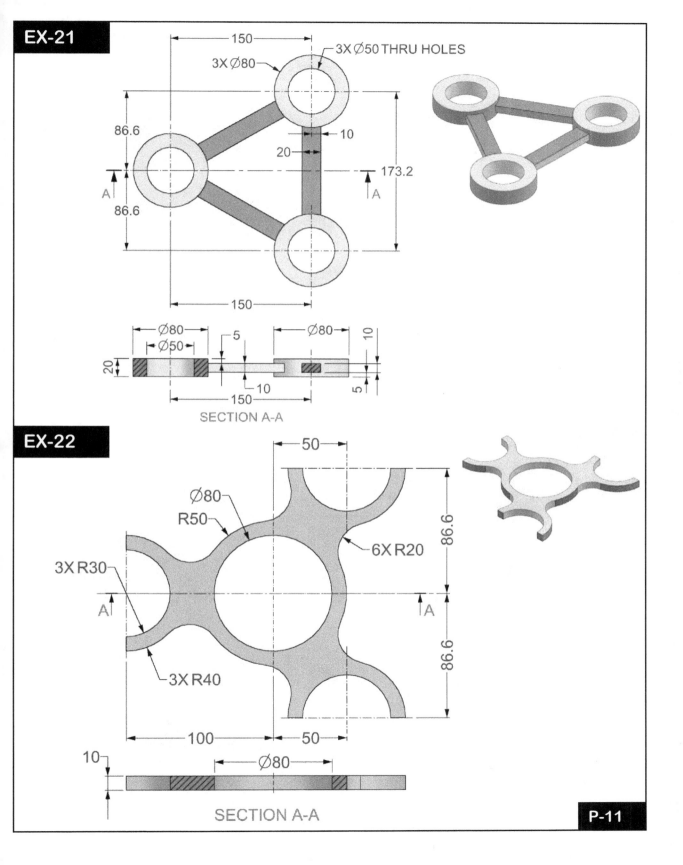

EX-21

150

3X Ø50 THRU HOLES

3X Ø80

86.6

10

20

173.2

A

A

86.6

150

Ø80
Ø50
5
Ø80
10
20
10
5
150

SECTION A-A

EX-22

50

Ø80

R50

86.6

6X R20

3X R30

A

A

86.6

3X R40

100

50

10

Ø80

SECTION A-A

P-11

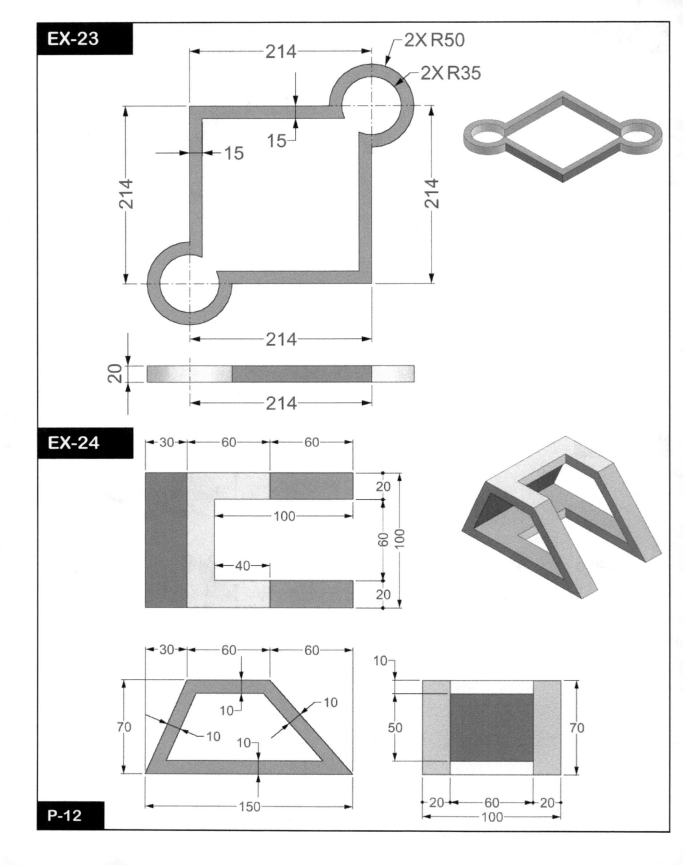

EX-23

214

2X R50
2X R35

15

15

214

214

214

20

214

EX-24

30 60 60

20
100
60
100
40
20

30 60 60

70
10
10
10
10
10

150

10
50
70

20 60 20
100

P-12

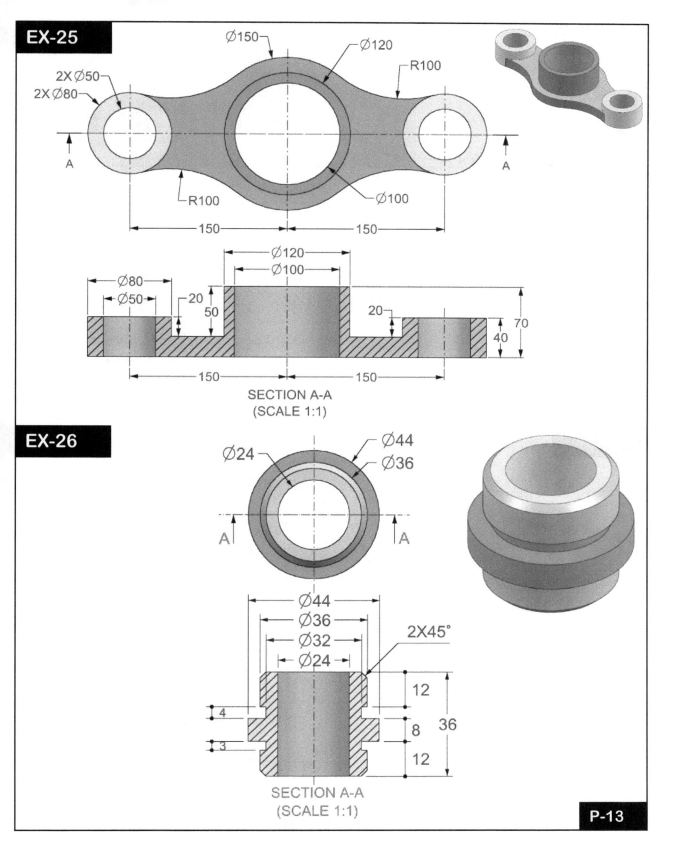

EX-25

Ø150
Ø120
R100
2X Ø50
2X Ø80
R100
Ø100
150
150

Ø120
Ø100
Ø80
Ø50
20
50
20
70
40
150
150

SECTION A-A
(SCALE 1:1)

EX-26

Ø24
Ø44
Ø36

A   A

Ø44
Ø36
Ø32
Ø24
2X45°
12
4
8
36
3
12

SECTION A-A
(SCALE 1:1)

P-13

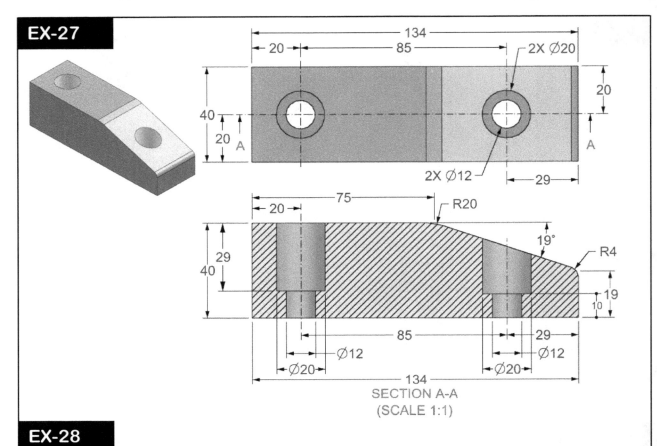

2X ⌀20

2X ⌀12

SECTION A-A
(SCALE 1:1)

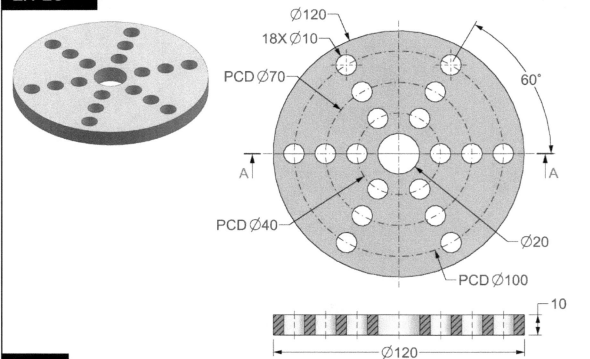

⌀120

18X ⌀10

PCD ⌀70

60°

PCD ⌀40

⌀20

PCD ⌀100

10

⌀120

SECTION A-A

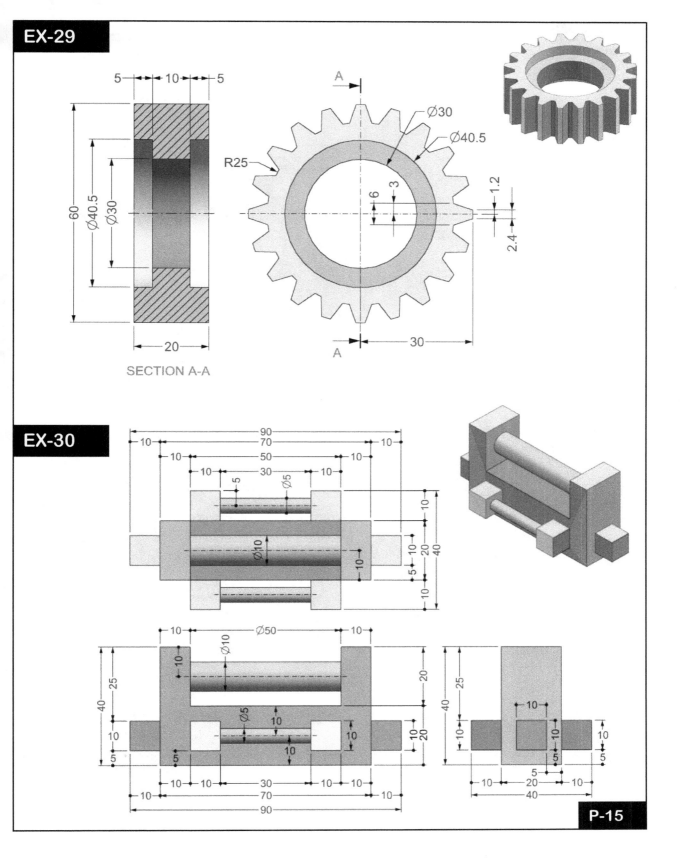

EX-29

SECTION A-A

EX-30

P-15

EX-31

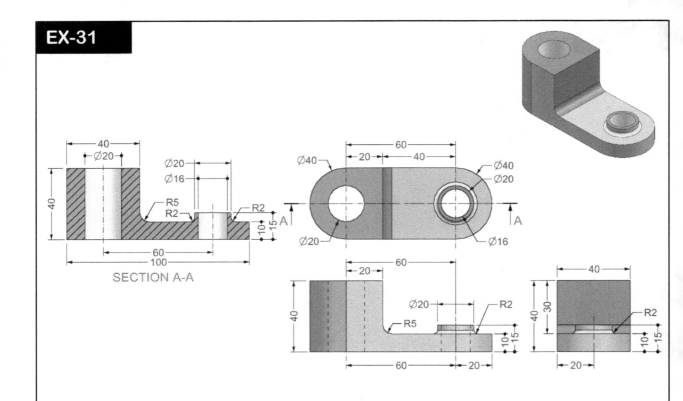

40
Ø20
Ø20
Ø16
R5
R2
R2
40
60
100
15
10
SECTION A-A

60
20
40
Ø40
Ø40
Ø20
Ø40
Ø20
Ø16
A
A

20
60
40
Ø20
R2
R5
15
10
60
20

40
30
40
R2
15
10
20

EX-32

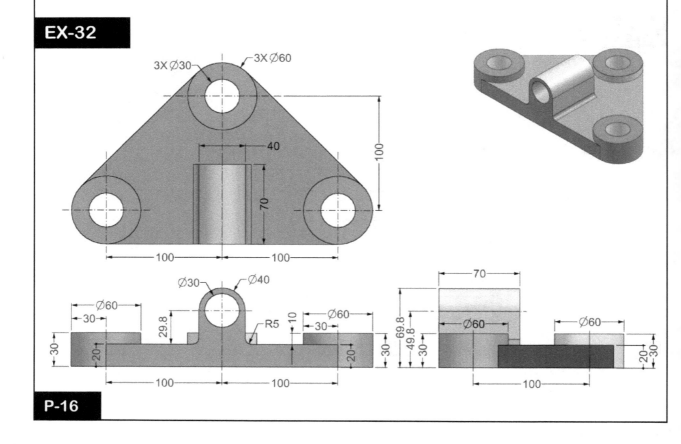

3X Ø30
3X Ø60
40
100
70
100
100

Ø30
Ø40
Ø60
30
29.8
R5
10
Ø60
30
30
20
100
100
20
30

70
69.8
49.8
30
Ø60
Ø60
20
30
100

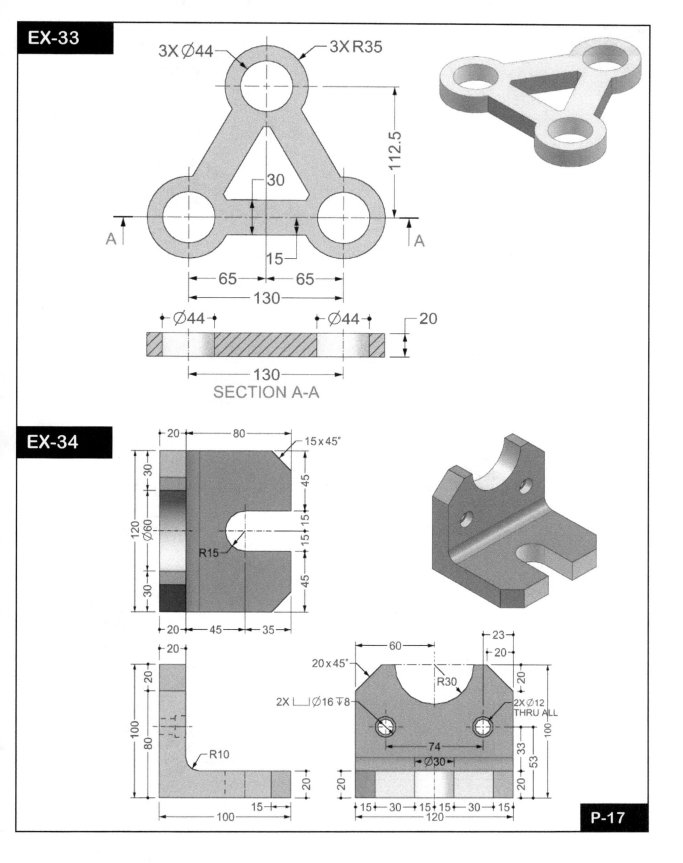

EX-33

3X⌀44   3X R35

112.5

30

A

A

15

65   65

130

⌀44   ⌀44   20

130

SECTION A-A

EX-34

20   80   15 x 45°

30

45

120   ⌀60   15   15

R15   15

30   45

20   45   35

20

20

100   80

R10

20

15

100

60   23

20

20 x 45°   R30   20

2X ⌴ ⌀16 ⫠8   2X ⌀12 THRU ALL

74   100

33

⌀30   53

20   20

15   30   15   15   30   15

120

P-17

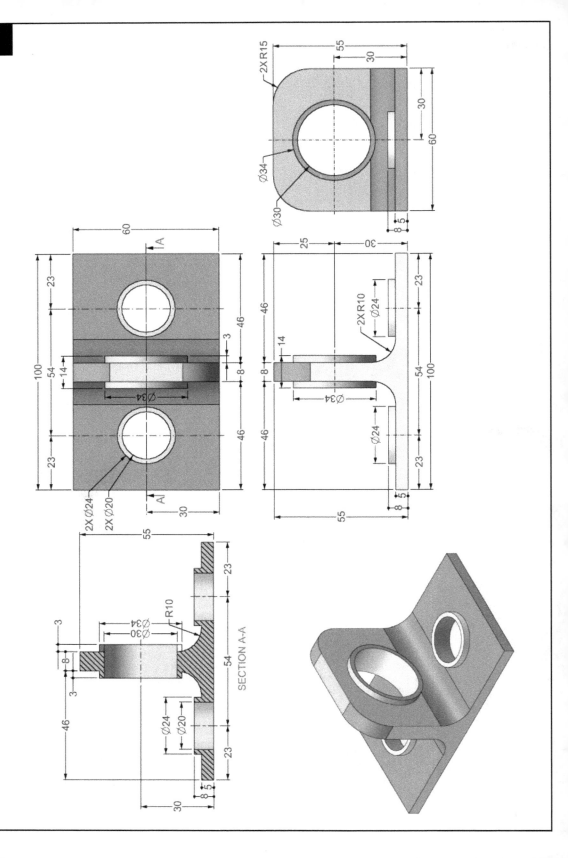

SECTION A-A

EX-36

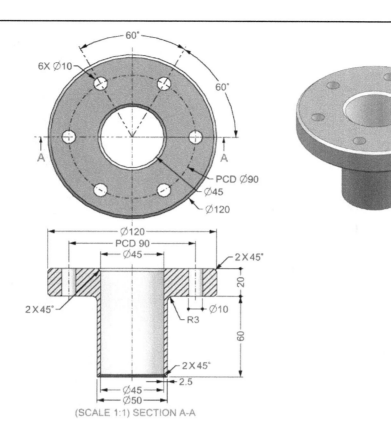

6X Ø10

60°

60°

PCD Ø90
Ø45
Ø120

Ø120
PCD 90
Ø45

2 X 45°

2 X 45°

20

Ø10

R3

60

2 X 45°

2.5

Ø45
Ø50

(SCALE 1:1) SECTION A-A

EX-37

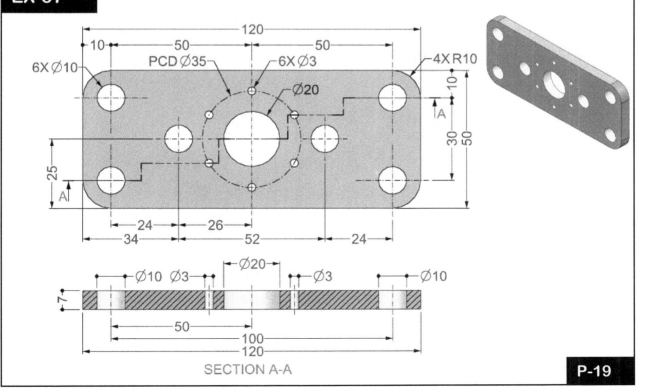

120

10

50

50

6X Ø10

PCD Ø35

6X Ø3

4X R10

Ø20

10

30

50

25

24

26

34

52

24

Ø20

Ø10 Ø3

Ø3

Ø10

7

50

100

120

SECTION A-A

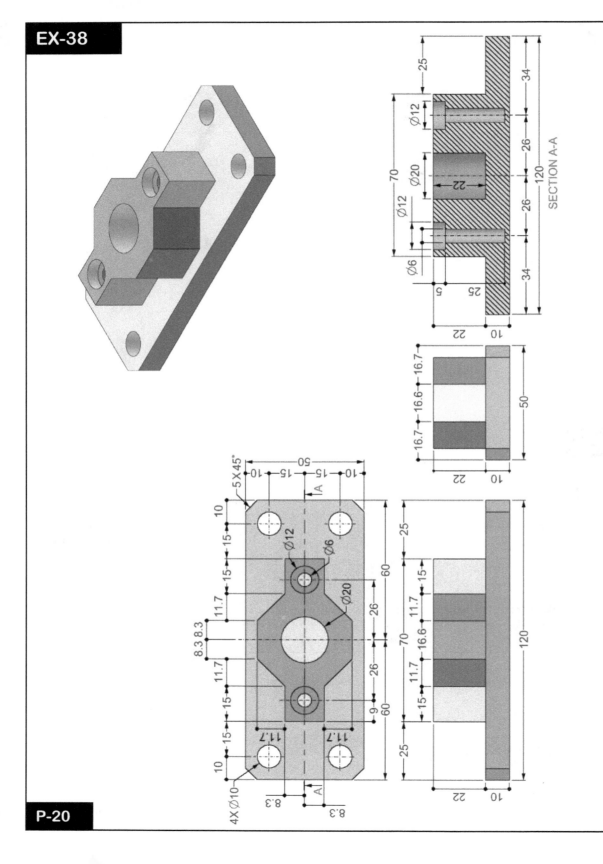

SECTION A-A

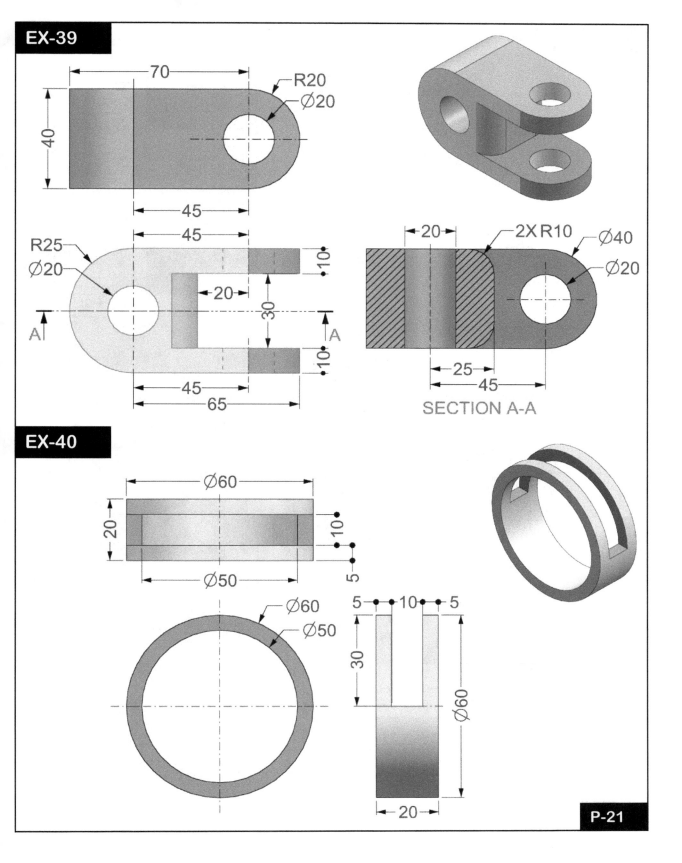

EX-39

70
R20
Ø20
40
45

45
R25
Ø20
20
30
A
A
45
65
10
10

20
2X R10
Ø40
Ø20
25
45
SECTION A-A

EX-40

Ø60
20
10
5
Ø50

Ø60
Ø50

5 10 5
30
Ø60
20

P-21

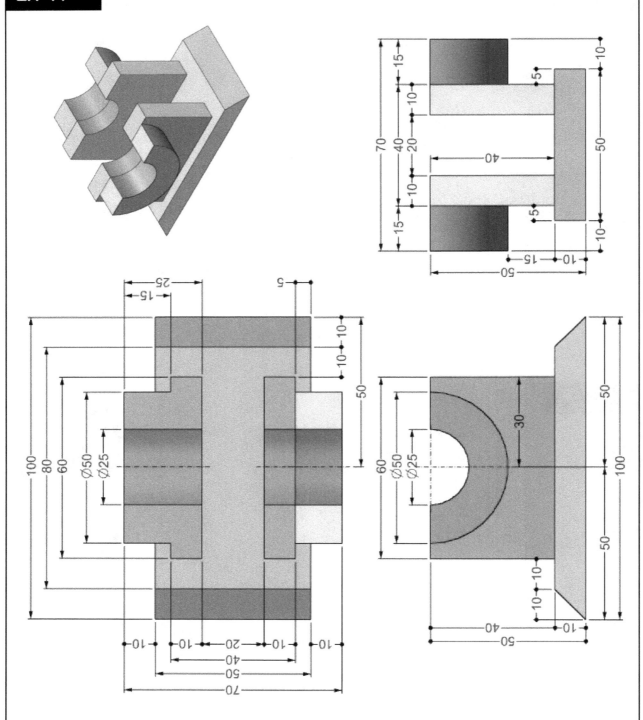

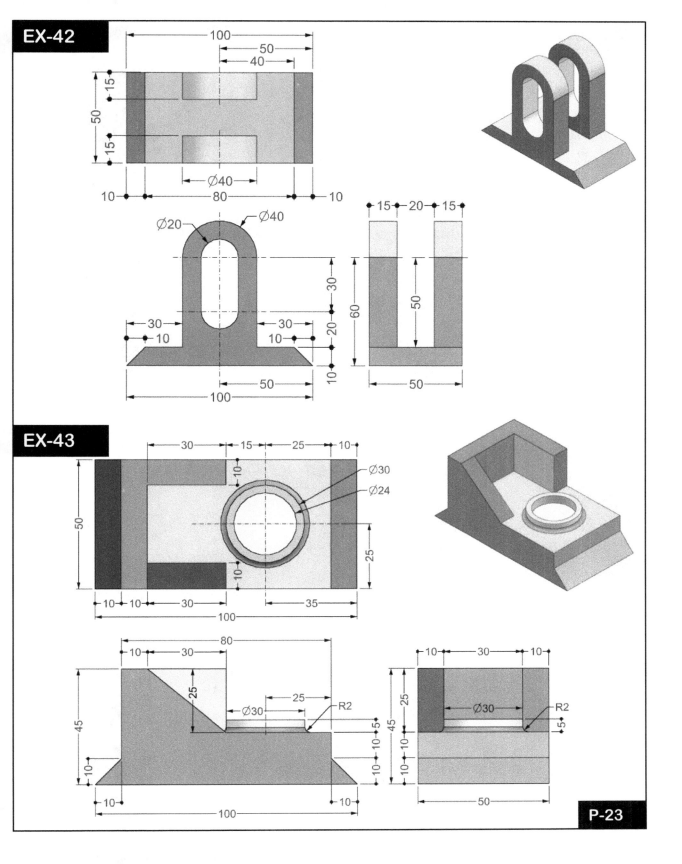

EX-42

EX-43

P-23

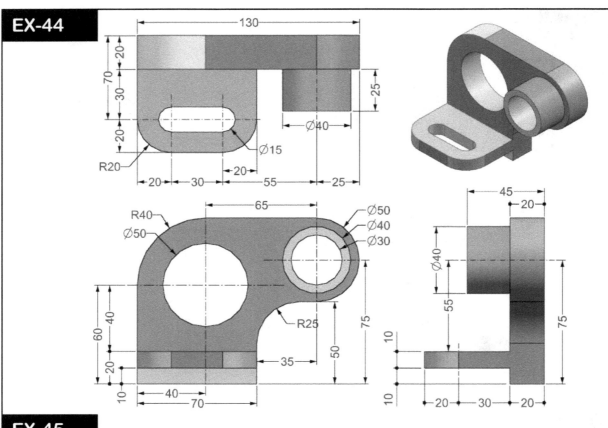

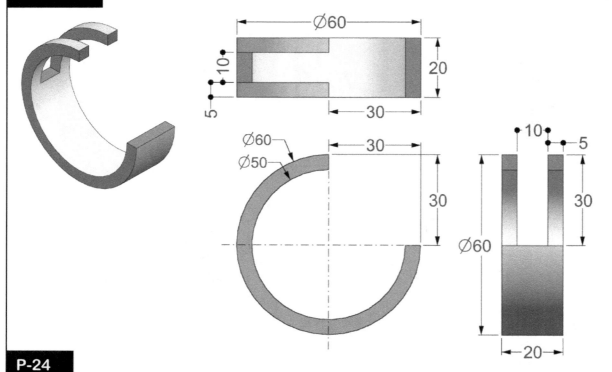

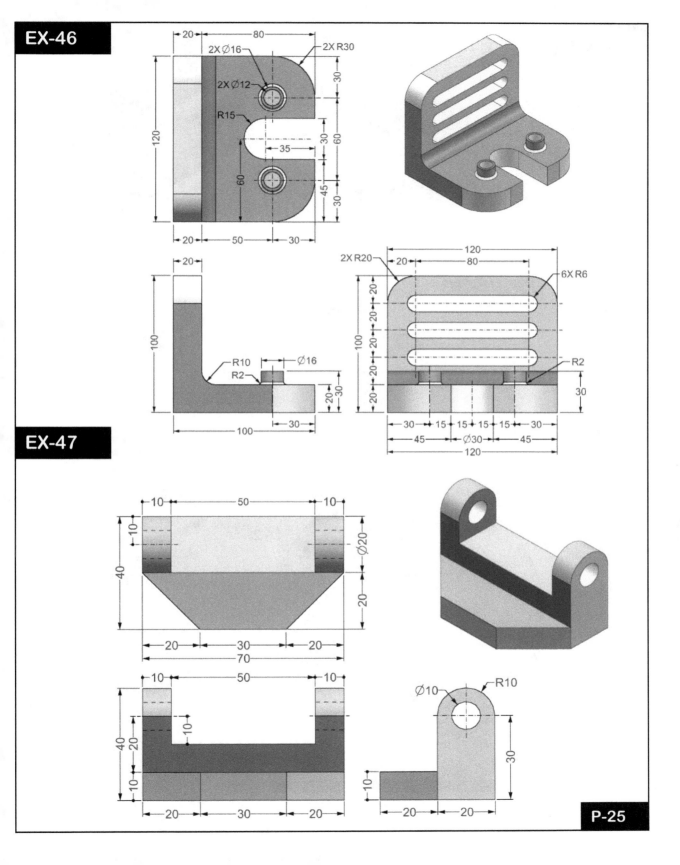

EX-46

EX-47

P-25

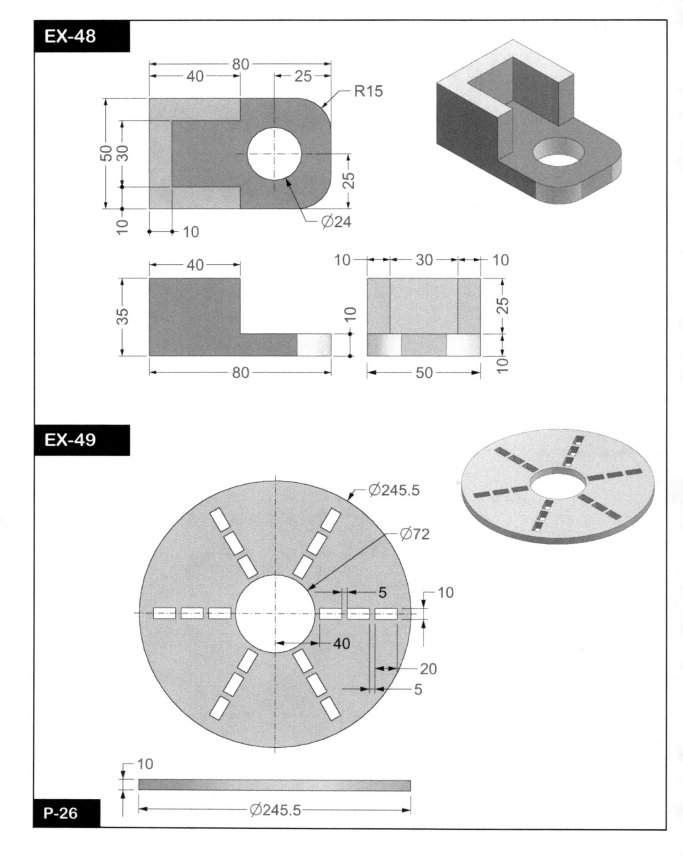

EX-48

EX-49

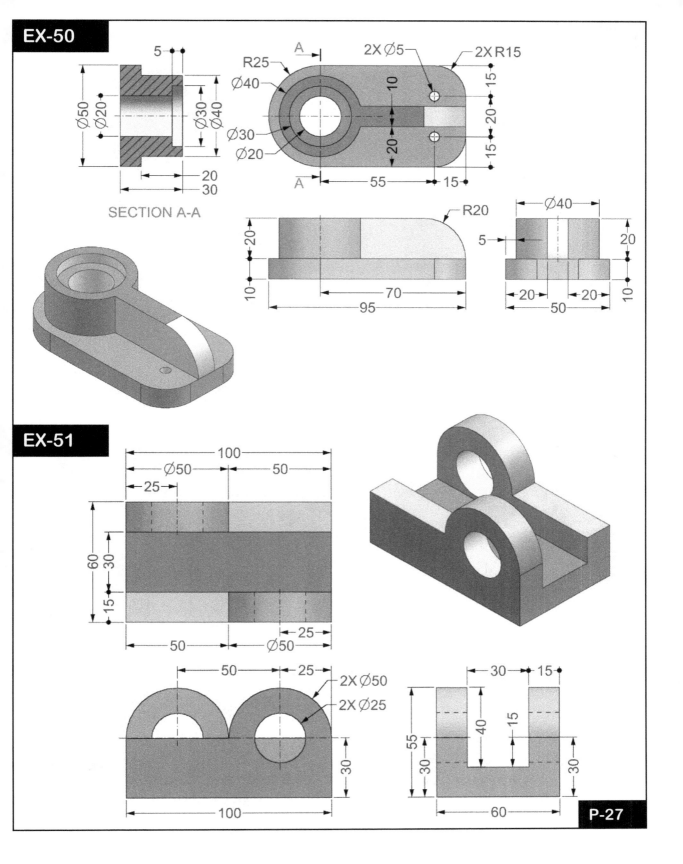

EX-50

SECTION A-A

2X Ø5 2X R15
R25
Ø40
Ø30
Ø20
Ø50 Ø20 Ø30 Ø40
5
10
15
20
15
20
55 15
R20
20
10
70
95
Ø40
5
20
20
20
50
10

EX-51

100
Ø50 50
25
60
30
15
50 Ø50
25

50 25
2X Ø50
2X Ø25
30
100

30 15
40
15
55
30
30
60

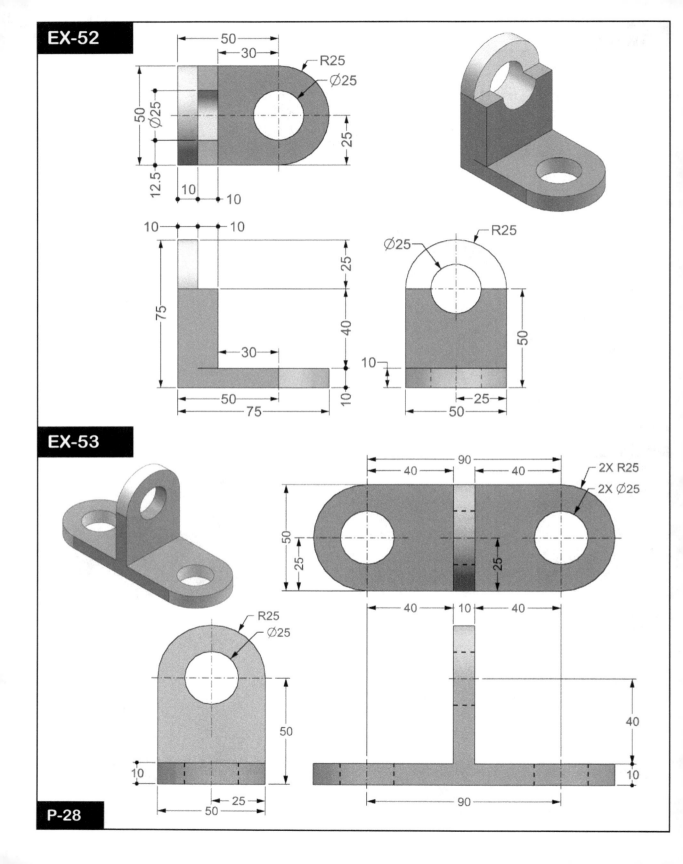

EX-52

EX-53

P-28

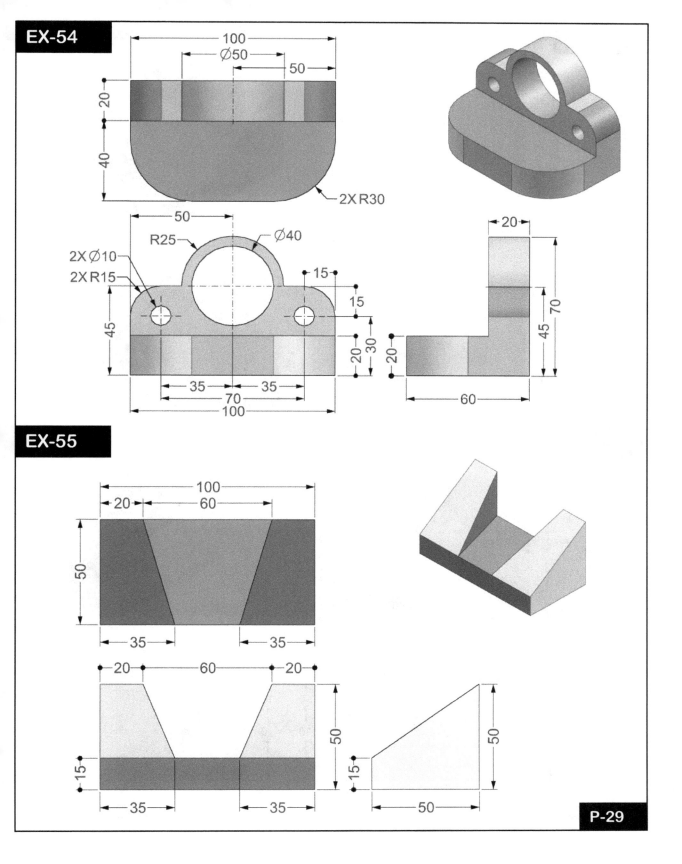

EX-54

100
Ø50
50
20
40
2X R30

50
R25
Ø40
2X Ø10
2X R15
45
15
15
35   35
70
100
20
30
20

20
70
45
20
60

EX-55

100
20   60
50
35   35

20   60   20
50
15
35   35

50
15
50

P-29

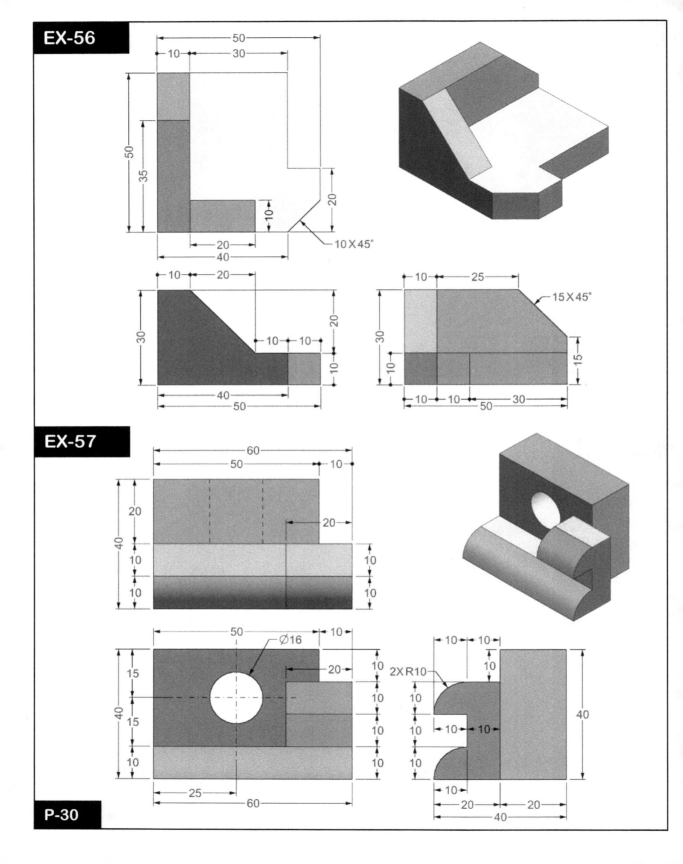

EX-56

EX-57

P-30

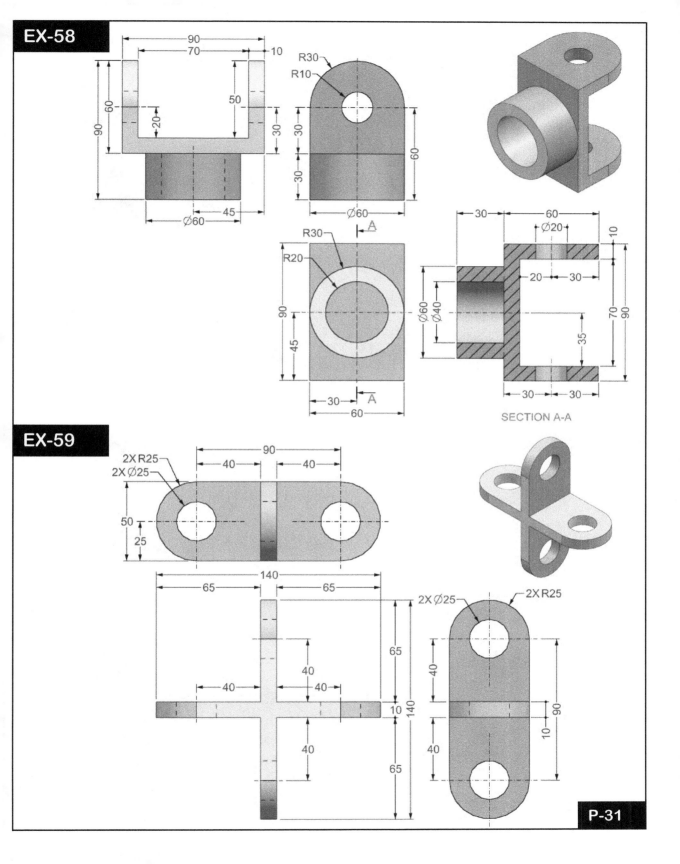

EX-58

90
70
10
60
90
50
20
30
30
45
Ø60

R30
R10
30
60
30
Ø60

R30
R20
90
45
30
60

30
60
Ø20
10
20
30
Ø60
Ø40
70
90
35
30
30

SECTION A-A

EX-59

2X R25
2X Ø25
90
40
40
50
25

140
65
65
65
40
40
40
10
140
40
65

2X Ø25
2X R25
40
90
10
40

P-31

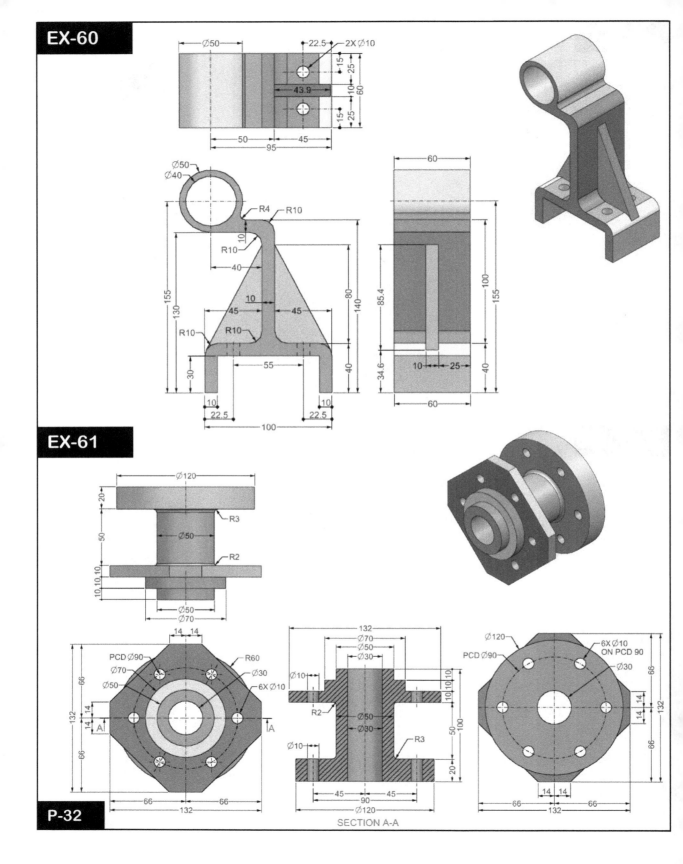

EX-60

EX-61

P-32

SECTION A-A

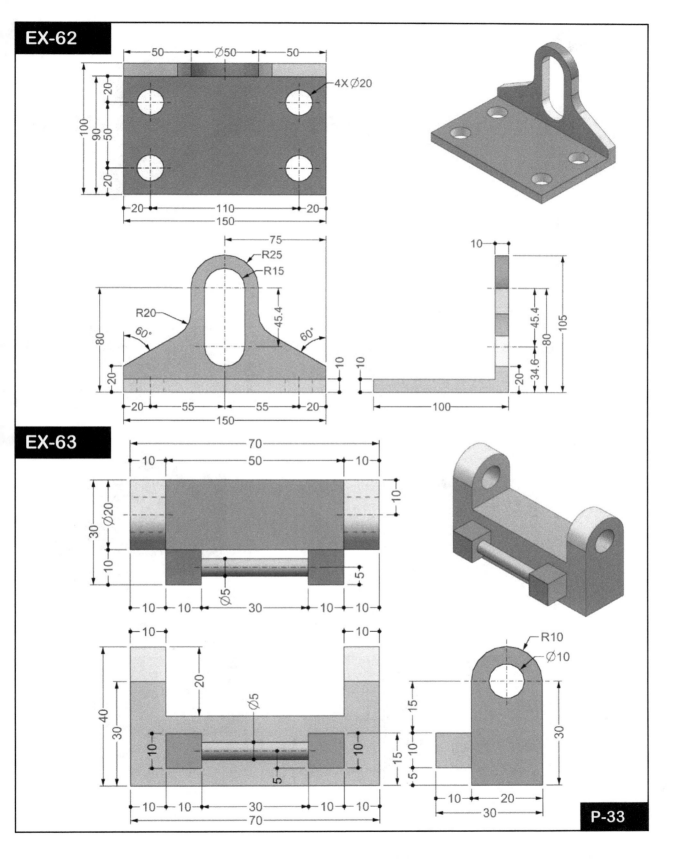

EX-62

50 Ø50 50

20
100
90
50
20

4X Ø20

20 110 20
150

75
R25
R15
R20
60° 60°
80
45.4
20 10
10
20 55 55 20
150

10
45.4
80
34.6
20
105
100

EX-63

70
10 50 10
10

Ø20
30
10

10 10 30 10 10

10 10

20
40
30
Ø5
10
5
15
10
5

10 10 30 10 10
70

R10
Ø10
15
10
5
30

10 20
30

P-33

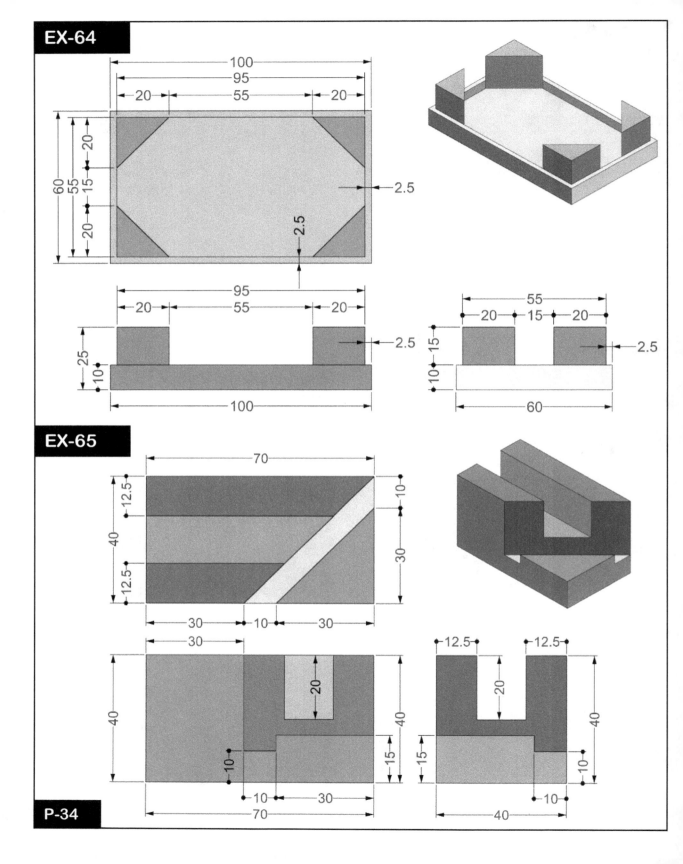

EX-64

EX-65

P-34

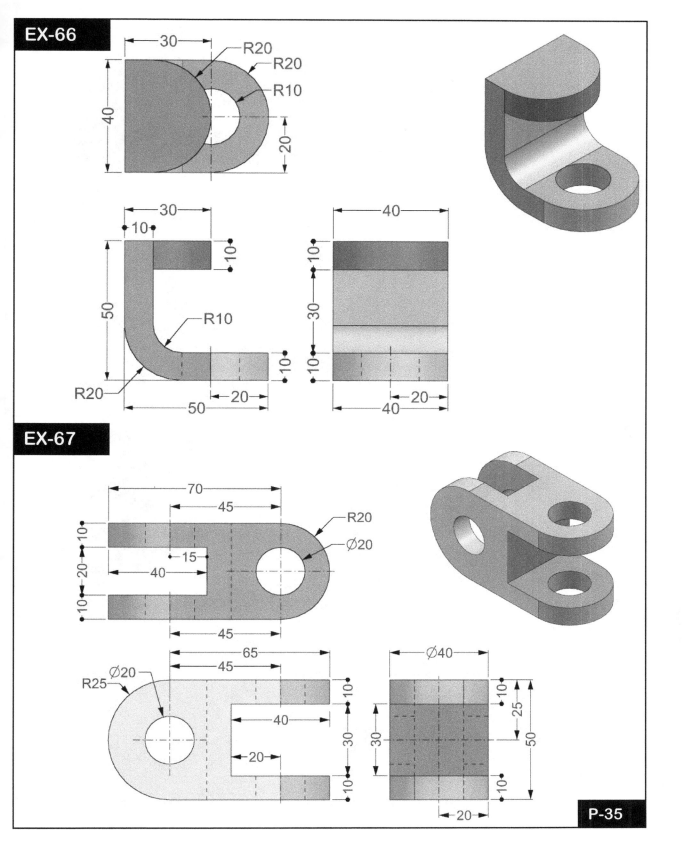

EX-66

EX-67

P-35

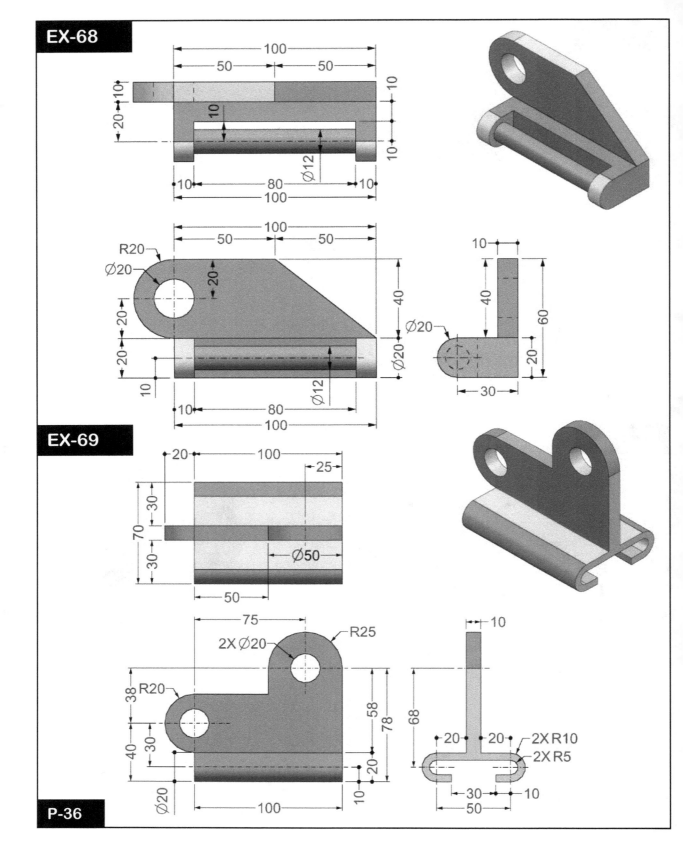

EX-68

EX-69

P-36

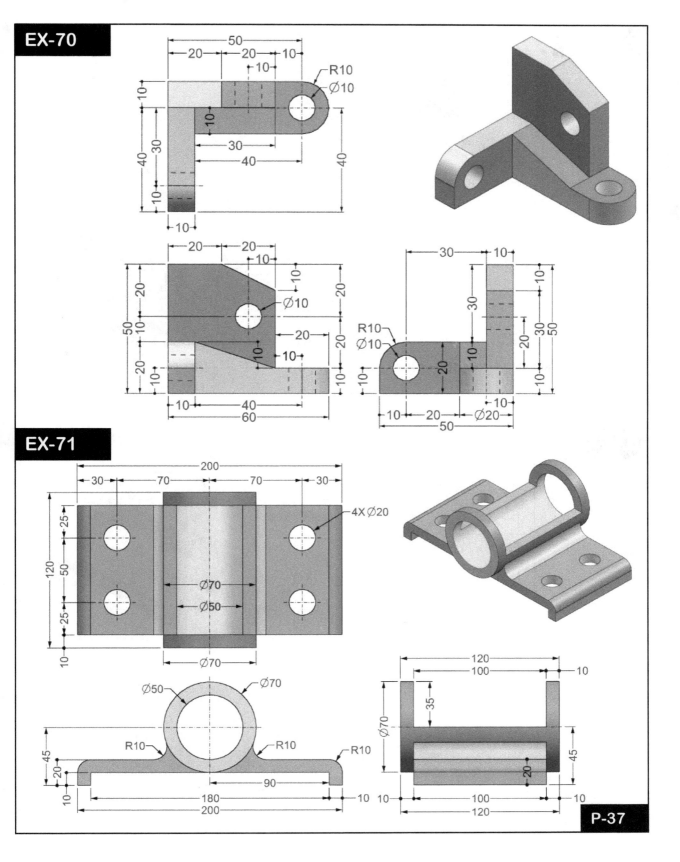

EX-70

EX-71

P-37

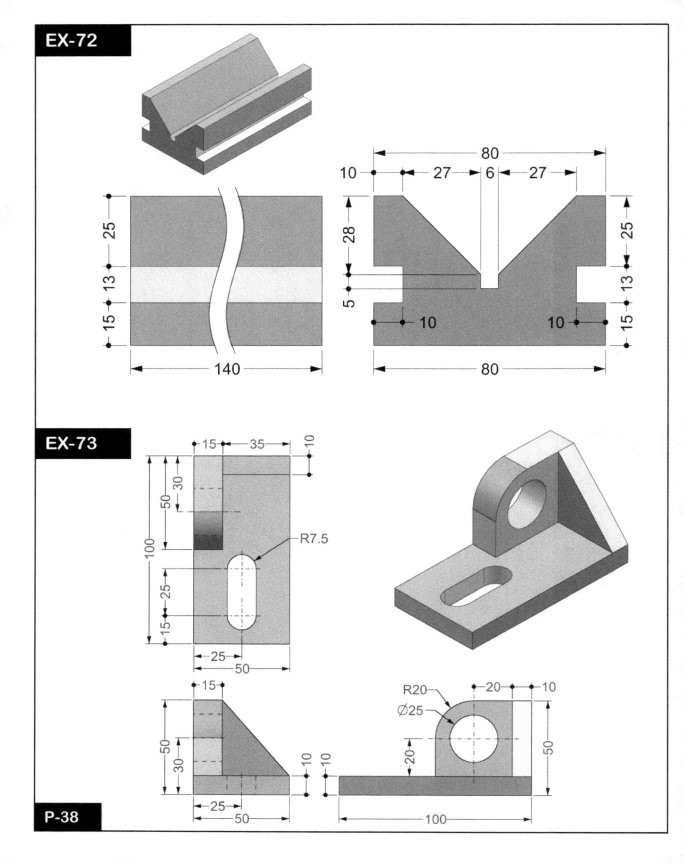

EX-72

EX-73

P-38

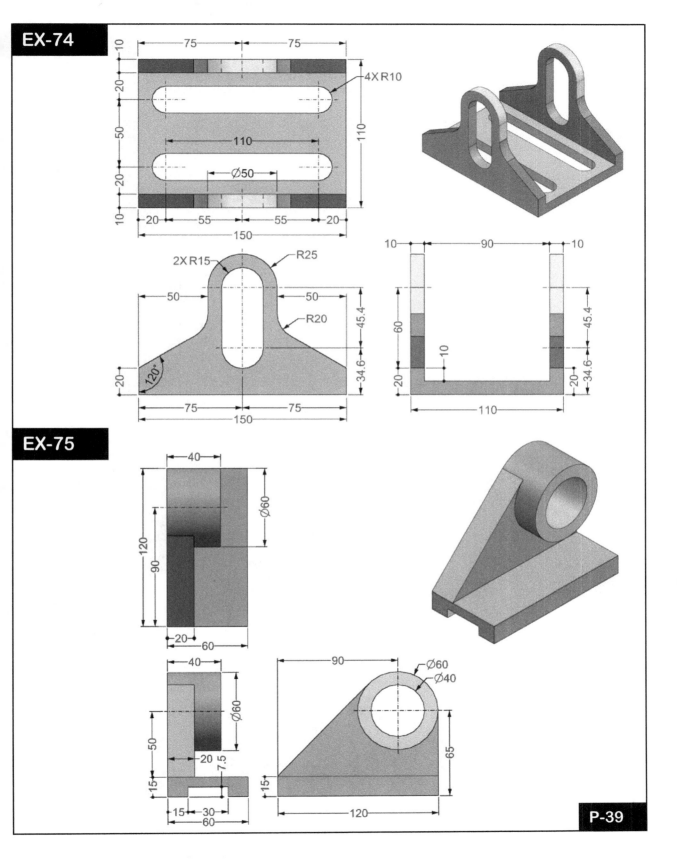

EX-74

4X R10

110

75 75

10 20 50 20 10

20 55 55 20

110

Ø50

150

2X R15 R25

50 50

R20

45.4

34.6

20

120°

75 75

150

10 90 10

60

10

20

45.4

34.6

20

110

EX-75

40

Ø60

120

90

20 60

40

Ø60

50

20 7.5

15

15 30

60

90 Ø60 Ø40

65

15

120

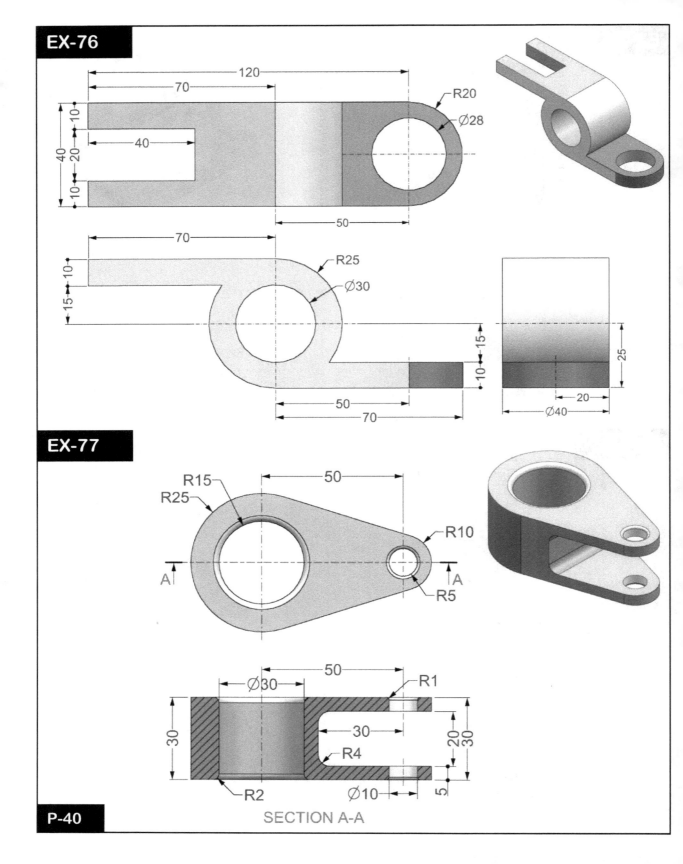

EX-76

EX-77

SECTION A-A

P-40

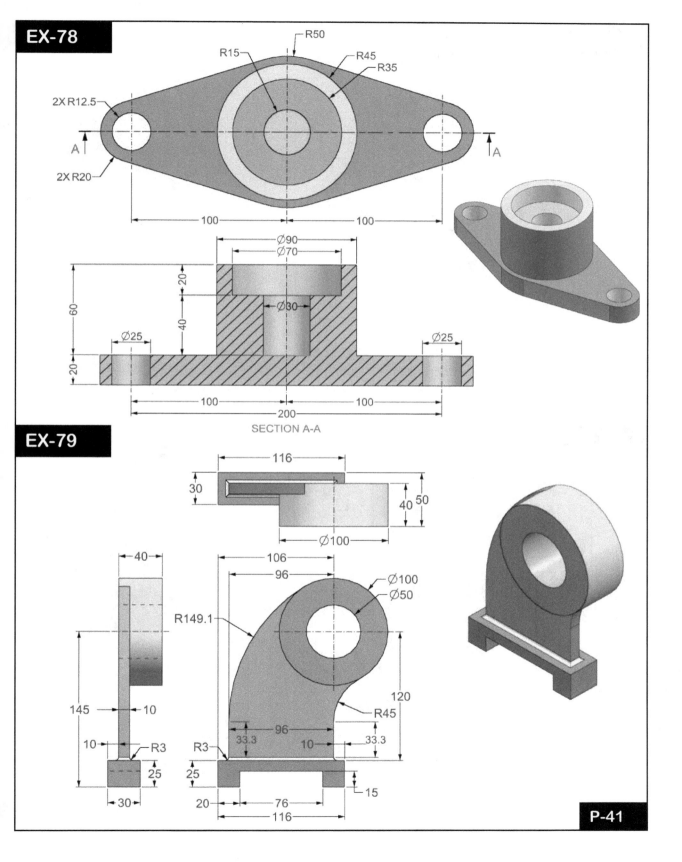

EX-78

R50
R15
R45
R35
2X R12.5
A
A
2X R20
100
100

Ø90
Ø70
20
60
40
Ø30
Ø25
Ø25
20
100
100
200

SECTION A-A

EX-79

116
30
40 50
Ø100

40
106
96
Ø100
Ø50
R149.1
145
10
120
R45
10
R3
96
R3
33.3
10
33.3
25
30
25
15
20
76
116

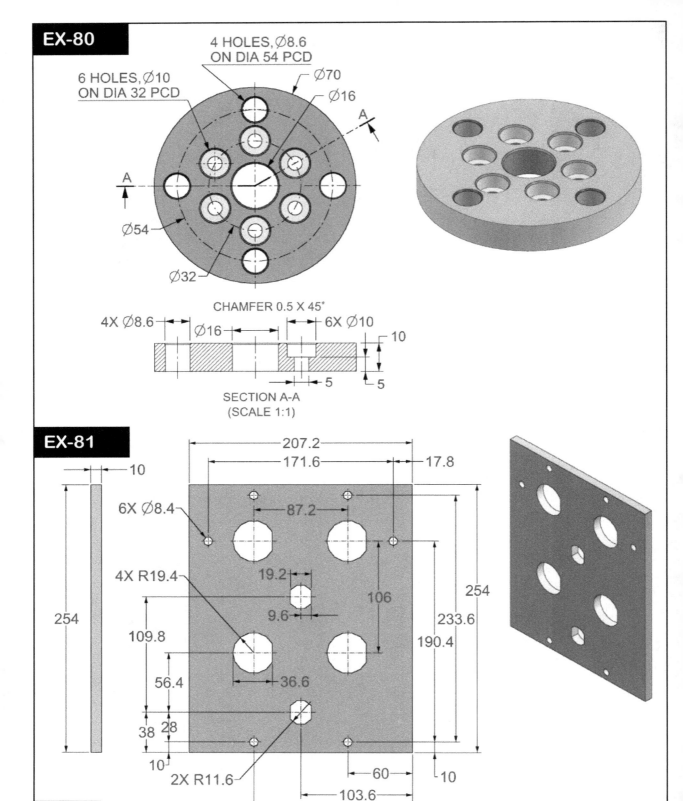

EX-80

6 HOLES,⌀10
ON DIA 32 PCD

4 HOLES,⌀8.6
ON DIA 54 PCD

⌀70

⌀16

A

A

⌀54

⌀32

CHAMFER 0.5 X 45°

4X ⌀8.6

⌀16

6X ⌀10

10

5

5

SECTION A-A
(SCALE 1:1)

EX-81

207.2

171.6

17.8

10

6X ⌀8.4

87.2

4X R19.4

19.2

9.6

106

254

233.6

190.4

109.8

56.4

36.6

38 28

2X R11.6

10

60

10

103.6

254

147.2

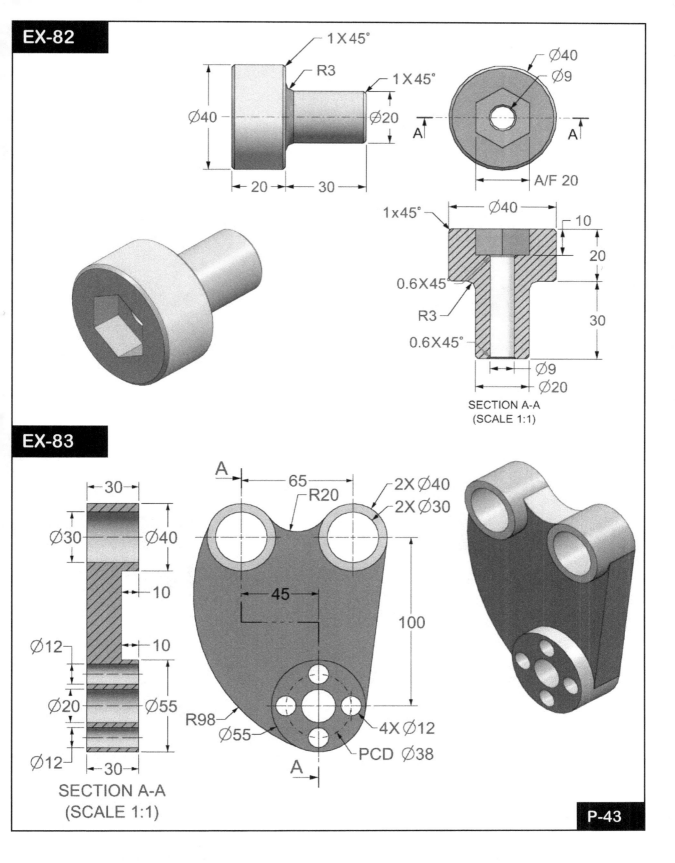

EX-82

1 X 45°
R3
1 X 45°
Ø40
Ø40
Ø9
Ø20
20
30
A/F 20

1x45°
Ø40
10
20
0.6X45°
R3
30
0.6X45°
Ø9
Ø20

SECTION A-A
(SCALE 1:1)

EX-83

30
Ø30
Ø40
10
10
Ø12
Ø20
Ø55
Ø12
30

SECTION A-A
(SCALE 1:1)

A
65
R20
2X Ø40
2X Ø30
45
100
R98
Ø55
4X Ø12
PCD Ø38
A

P-43

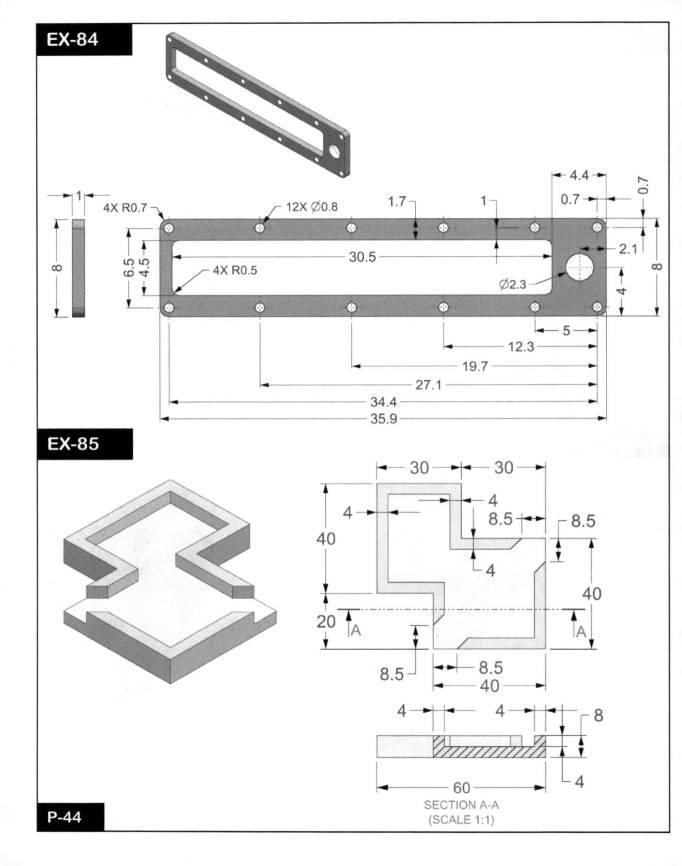

EX-84

4X R0.7   12X Ø0.8   1.7   1   4.4   0.7   0.7

1   8   6.5   4.5   4X R0.5   30.5   2.1   Ø2.3   8   4

5   12.3   19.7   27.1   34.4   35.9

EX-85

30   30   4   4   8.5   8.5

40   4   8.5   4   40

20   A   8.5   8.5   A   40

4   4   8

60

SECTION A-A
(SCALE 1:1)

P-44

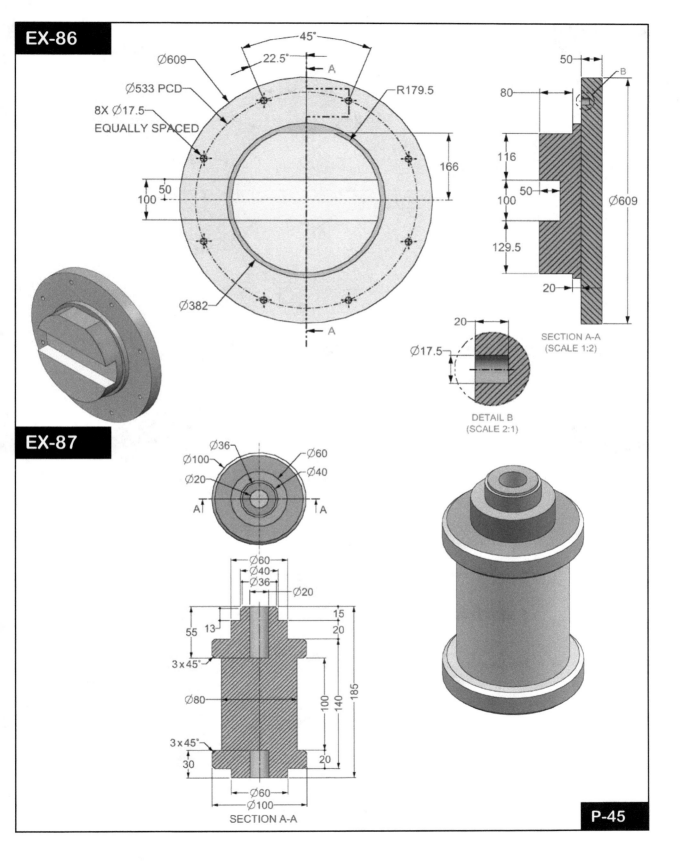

EX-86

Ø609
Ø533 PCD
8X Ø17.5
EQUALLY SPACED
45°
22.5°
A
R179.5
166
50
100
Ø382
A

50
80
B
116
50
100
Ø609
129.5
20
SECTION A-A
(SCALE 1:2)

20
Ø17.5
DETAIL B
(SCALE 2:1)

EX-87

Ø36
Ø100
Ø20
Ø60
Ø40
A
A

Ø60
Ø40
Ø36
Ø20
15
55
13
20
3 x 45°
Ø80
100
140
185
3 x 45°
30
20
Ø60
Ø100
SECTION A-A

P-45

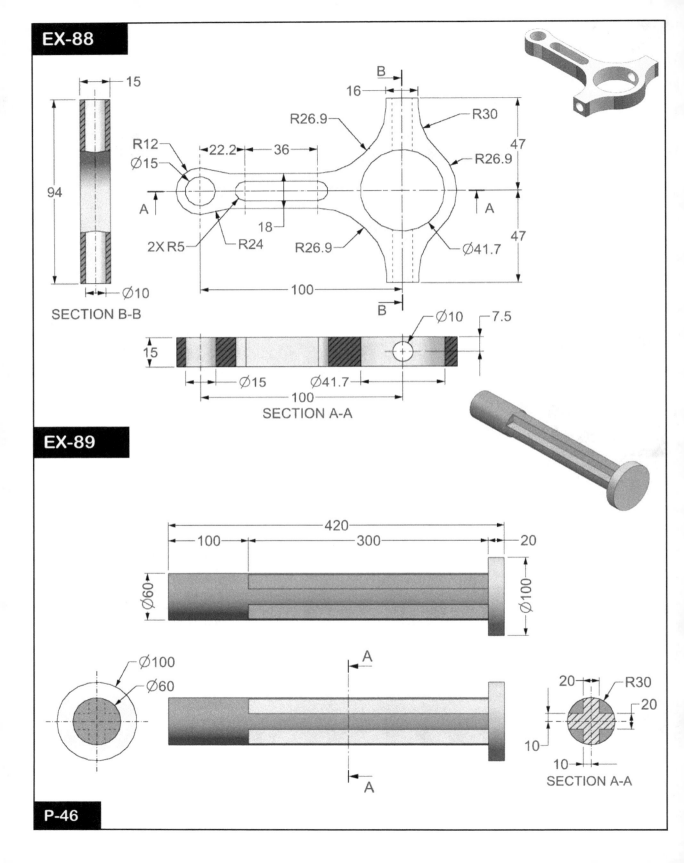

EX-88

94

15

SECTION B-B

Ø10

R12
Ø15

22.2 36

R26.9

B

16

R30

47

R26.9

A

A

47

2X R5   R24

18

R26.9

Ø41.7

100

B

Ø10   7.5

15

Ø15   Ø41.7

100

SECTION A-A

EX-89

420

100   300   20

Ø60

Ø100

Ø100
Ø60

A

A

20   R30

20

10

10

SECTION A-A

P-46

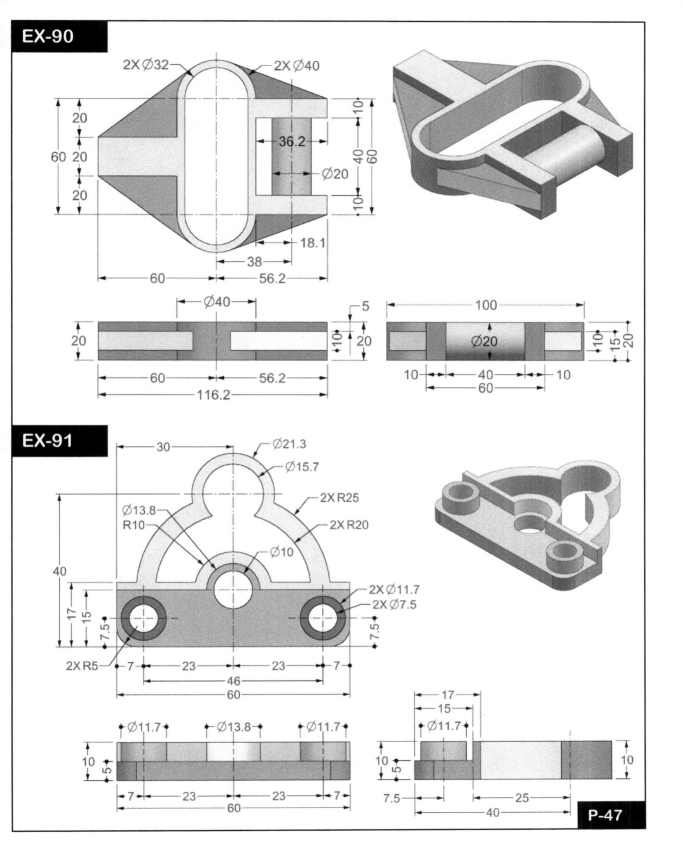

EX-90

2X Ø32   2X Ø40

60   20 20 20

10 40 60 10

36.2
Ø20

18.1
38
60   56.2

Ø40
20   5
10   20
60   56.2
116.2

100
Ø20
10   40   10
60
10 15 20

EX-91

30   Ø21.3
Ø15.7

Ø13.8
R10   2X R25
2X R20
Ø10

40
17
15
7.5

2X Ø11.7
2X Ø7.5

2X R5   7   23   23   7
46
60

Ø11.7   Ø13.8   Ø11.7
10
5
7   23   23   7
60

17
15
Ø11.7
10
5
7.5   25
40
10

P-47

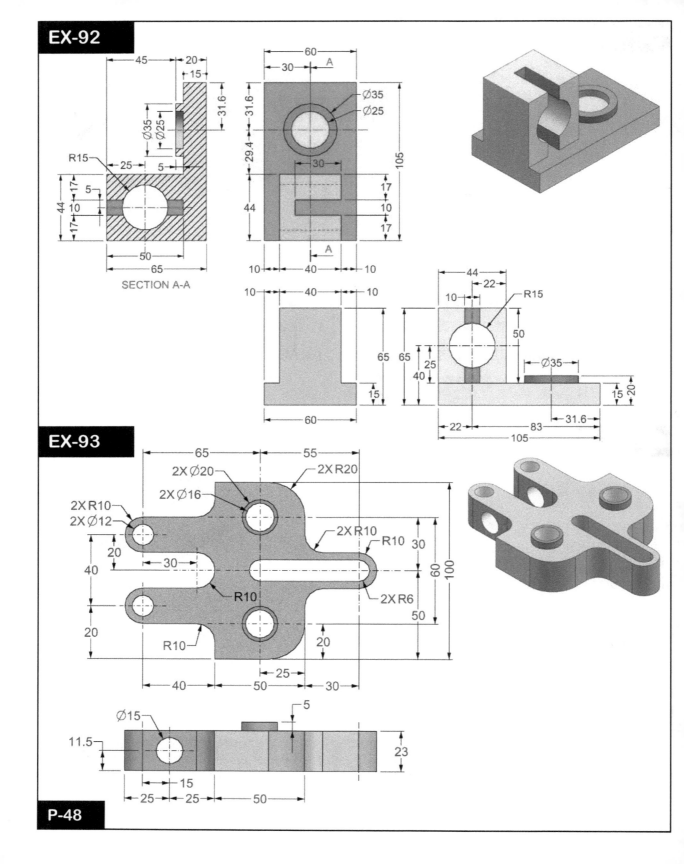

EX-92

SECTION A-A

EX-93

P-48

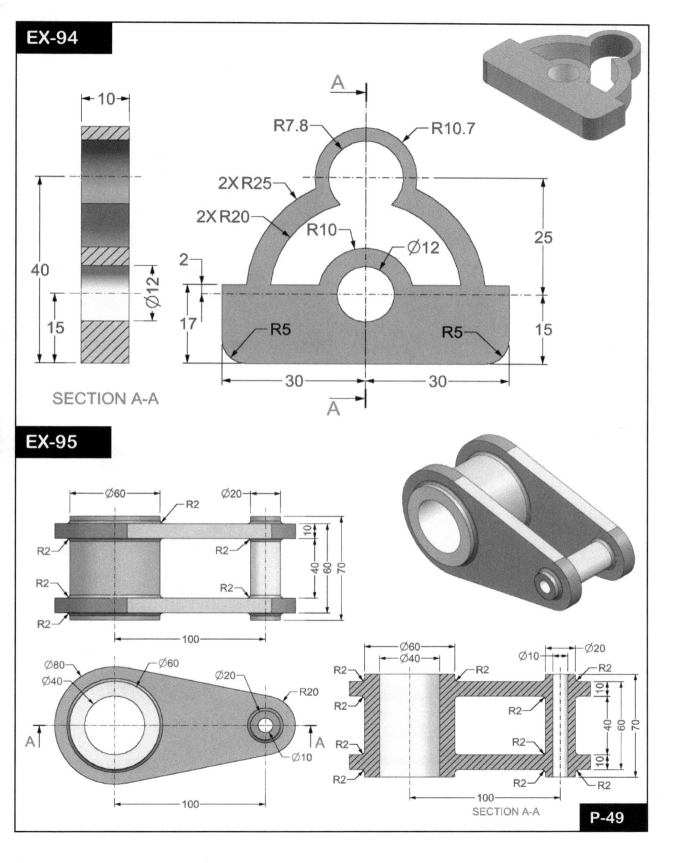

EX-94

R7.8 R10.7

2X R25

2X R20 R10 Ø12

25

2 40 Ø12

15

17 R5 R5

15

30 30

10

SECTION A-A

EX-95

Ø60 Ø20 R2

R2 R2

10

40 60 70

R2 R2

100

Ø80 Ø60 Ø20

Ø40 R20

Ø10

100

Ø60 Ø10 Ø20

Ø40 R2 R2

R2 R2

10

R2 R2 40 60 70

10

R2 R2

100

SECTION A-A

P-49

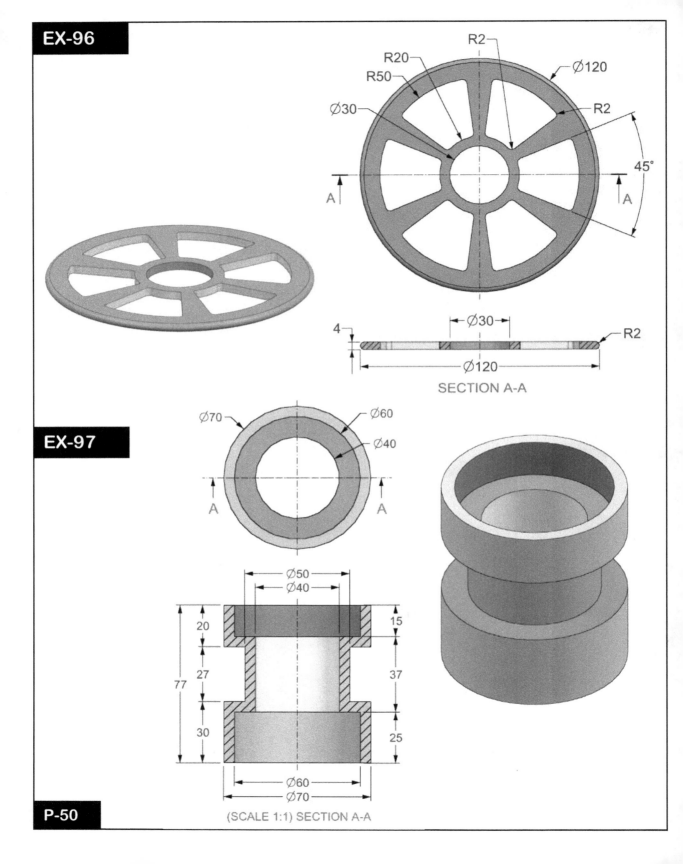

EX-96

R2
R20
R50
⌀30
⌀120
R2
45°
A
A

⌀30
4
⌀120
R2
SECTION A-A

EX-97

⌀70
⌀60
⌀40
A
A

⌀50
⌀40
20
15
77
27
37
30
25
⌀60
⌀70

P-50

(SCALE 1:1) SECTION A-A

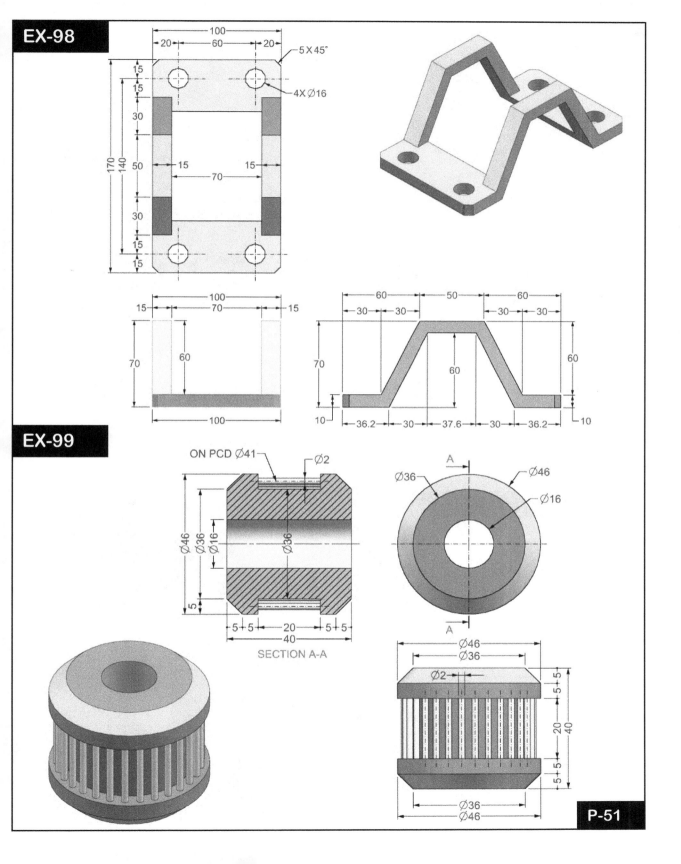

EX-98

EX-99

ON PCD Ø41

SECTION A-A

P-51

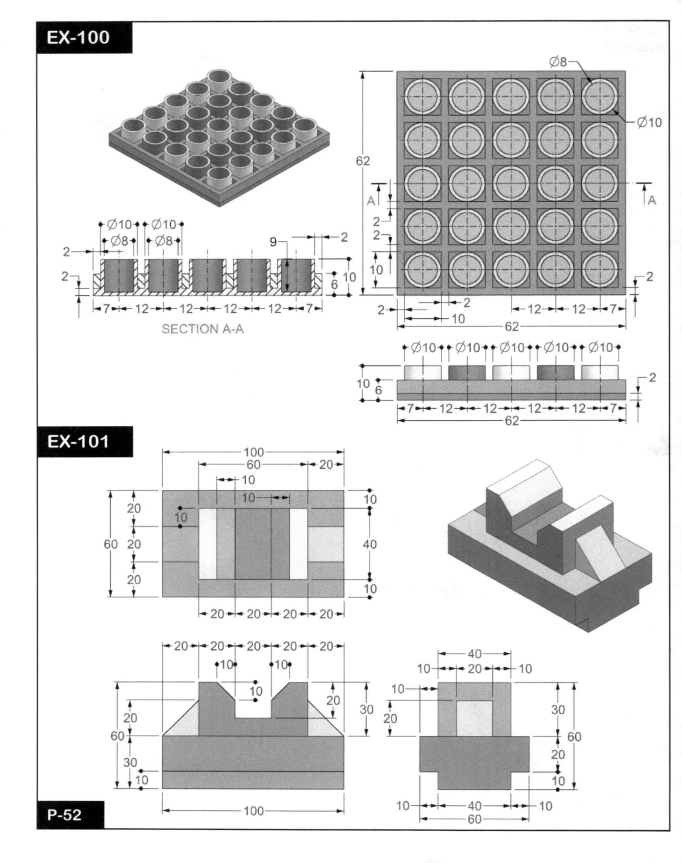

EX-100

Ø8
Ø10

62

A | A

2
2

10

2
10
62
12 12 7

Ø10 Ø10
Ø8 Ø8
2
2
9
2

10
6

7 12 12 12 12 7

SECTION A-A

Ø10 Ø10 Ø10 Ø10 Ø10

10
6
2

7 12 12 12 12 7
62

EX-101

100
60 20
10
10
10
20
10
60 20
40
20
10
20 20 20 20

20 20 20 20 20
10 10
10
20
30
20
20
60
30
10
100

40
10 20 10
10
10
30
20
60
20
10
10 40 10
60

P-52

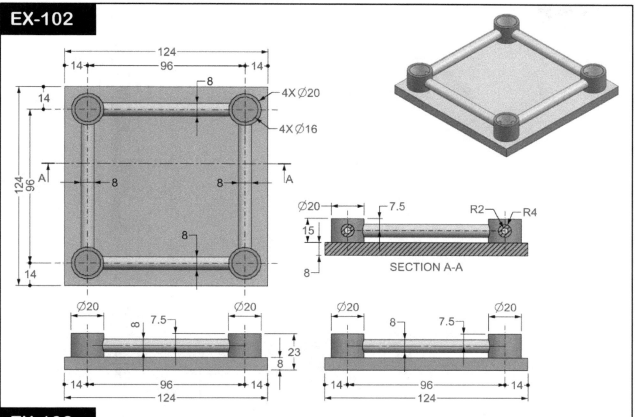

SECTION A-A

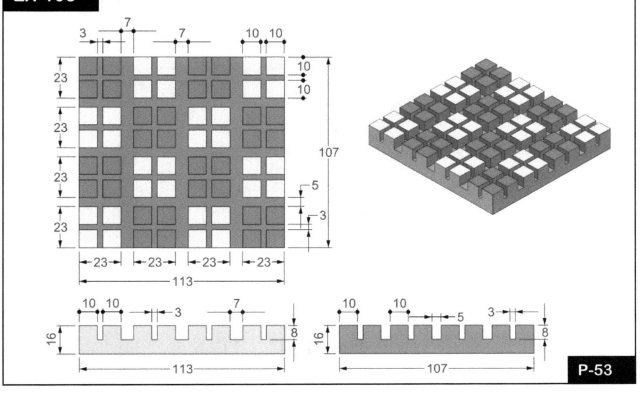

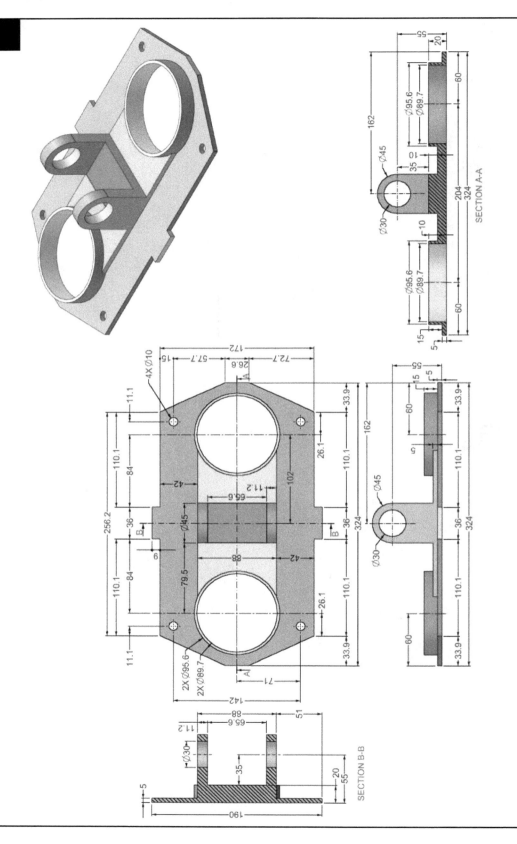

SECTION A-A

SECTION B-B

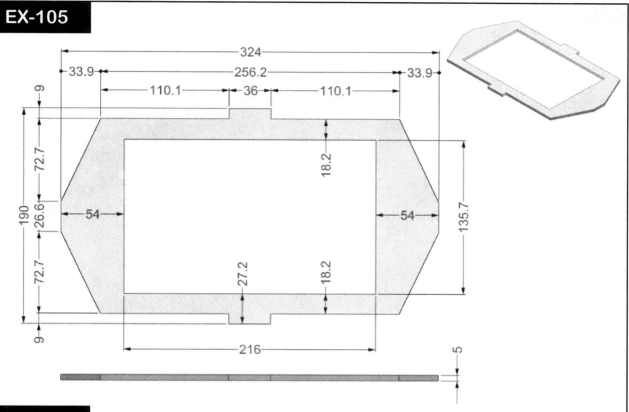

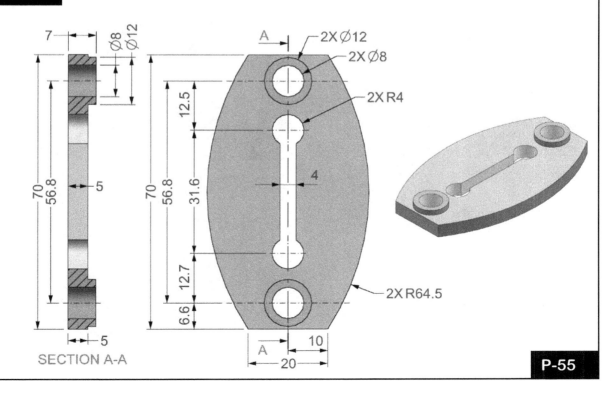

SECTION A-A

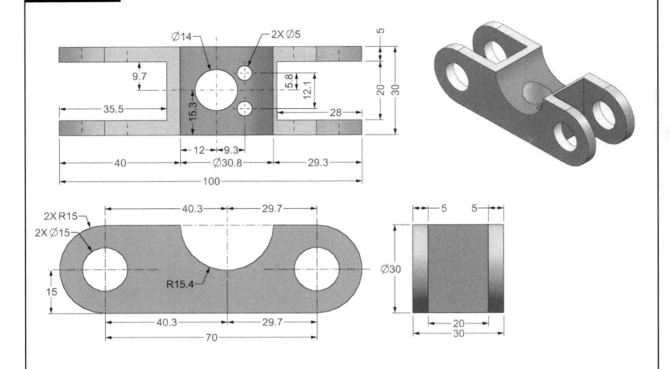

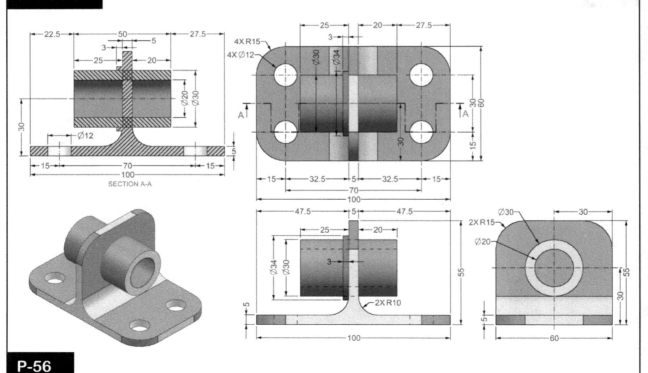

SECTION A-A

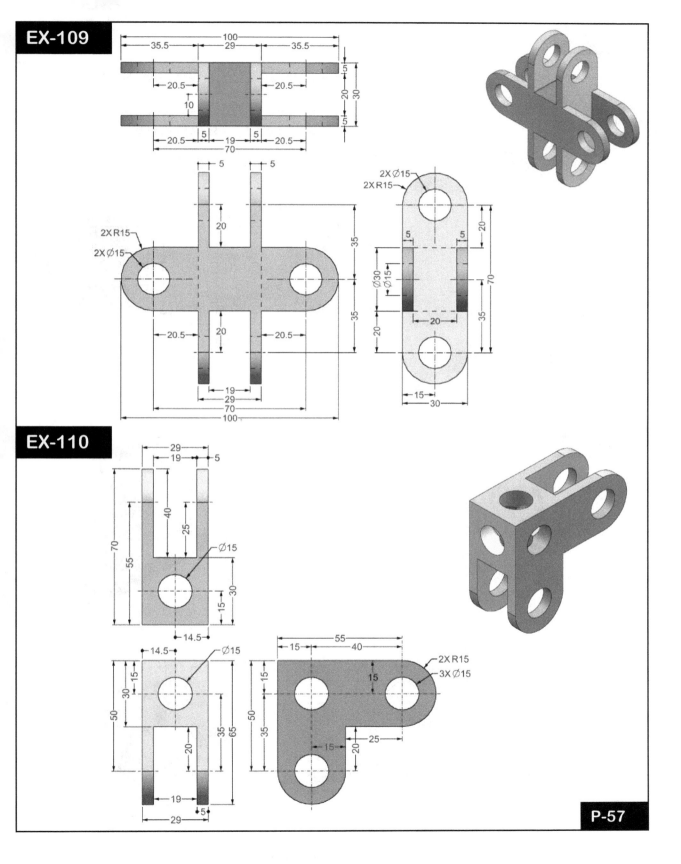

EX-109

EX-110

EX-111

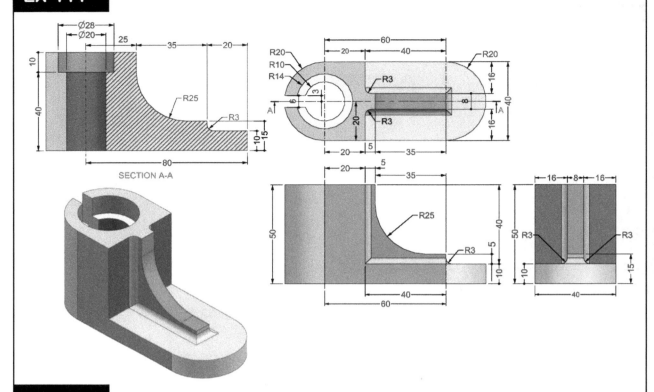

SECTION A-A

EX-112

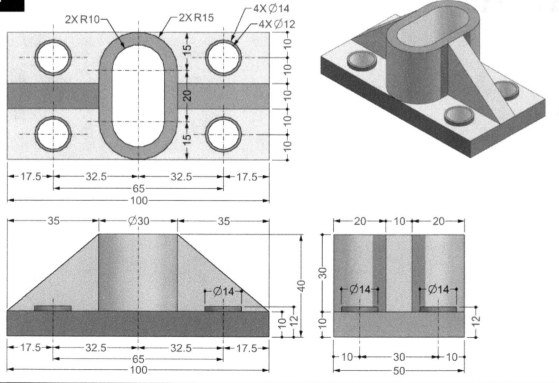

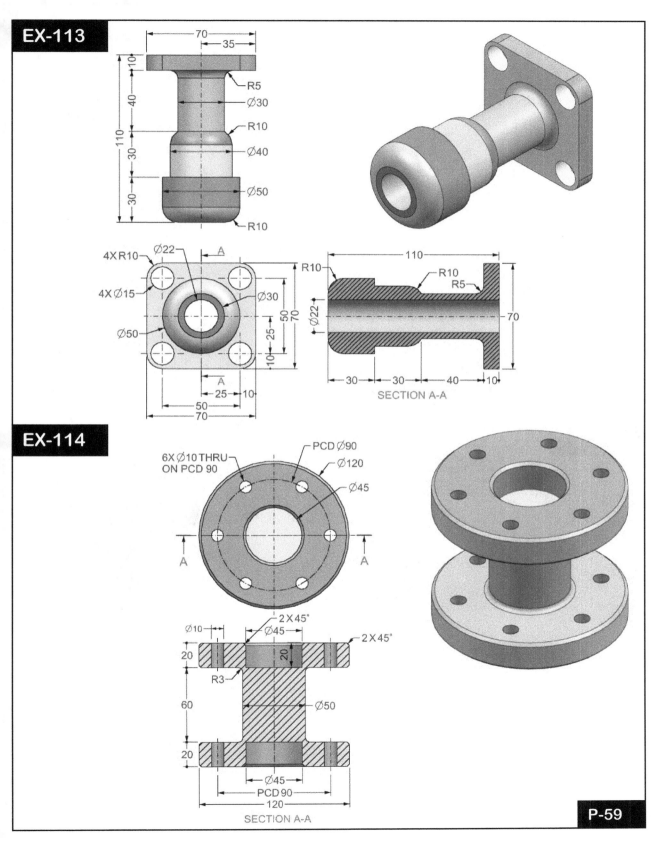

EX-113

70
35
10
40
110
30
30

R5
Ø30
R10
Ø40
Ø50
R10

4X R10
Ø22
A
4X Ø15
Ø30
Ø50
50
70
25
10
A
25
10
50
70

R10
110
R10
R5
Ø22
70
30
30
40
10
SECTION A-A

EX-114

6X Ø10 THRU
ON PCD 90
PCD Ø90
Ø120
Ø45

A
A

Ø10
2 X 45°
Ø45
20
20
R3
2 X 45°
60
Ø50
20
Ø45
PCD 90
120
SECTION A-A

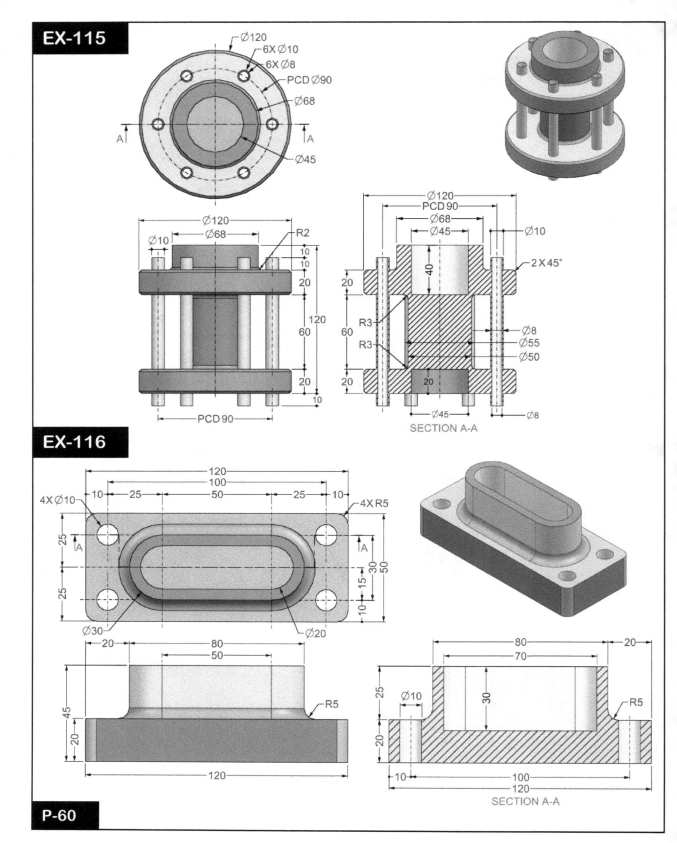

EX-115

∅120
6X ∅10
6X ∅8
PCD ∅90
∅68
∅45

A   A

∅120
∅68
R2
∅10
10
10
20
20
120
60
20
10
PCD 90

∅120
PCD 90
∅68
∅45
∅10
2 X 45°
40
20
R3
60
R3
∅8
∅55
∅50
20
20
∅45
∅8

SECTION A-A

EX-116

120
100
10   25   50   25   10
4X ∅10
4X R5
25
A   A
25
30   50
15
10
∅30
∅20

20
80
50
45
20
R5
120

80   20
70
25
∅10
30
R5
20
10
100
120

SECTION A-A

P-60

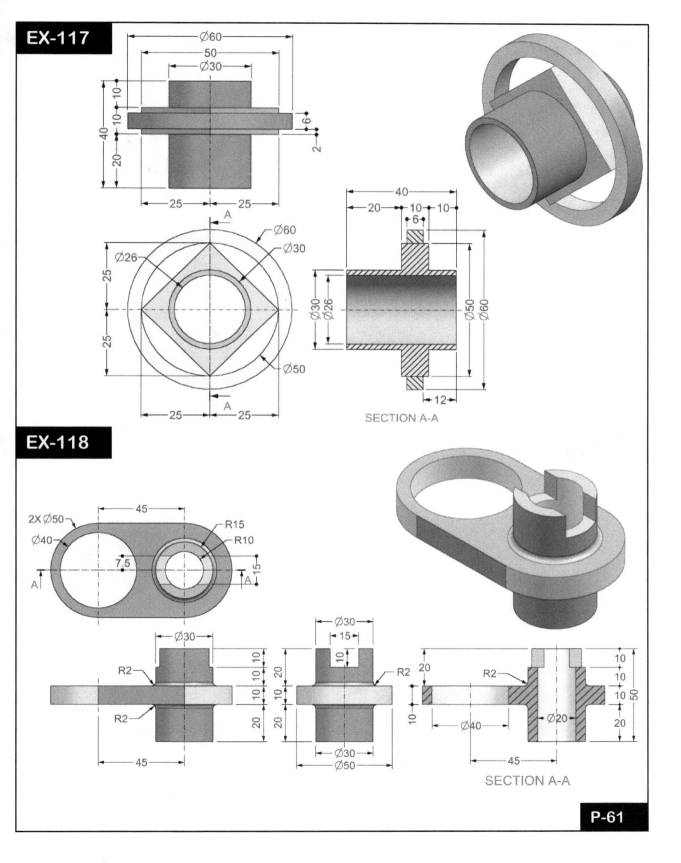

EX-117

Ø60
50
Ø30
10
10
40
20
25   25
A

Ø60
Ø30
Ø26
25
25
Ø50
25   25
A

40
20   10   10
6
Ø30
Ø26
Ø50
Ø60
12
SECTION A-A

EX-118

45
2X Ø50
Ø40
R15
R10
7.5
15
A   A

Ø30
R2
10 10
10 10
R2
20 20
45

Ø30
15
10
20 20
10 10
R2
Ø30
Ø50

20
R2
10
Ø40
Ø20
45
SECTION A-A

10
10
10
50
20

P-61

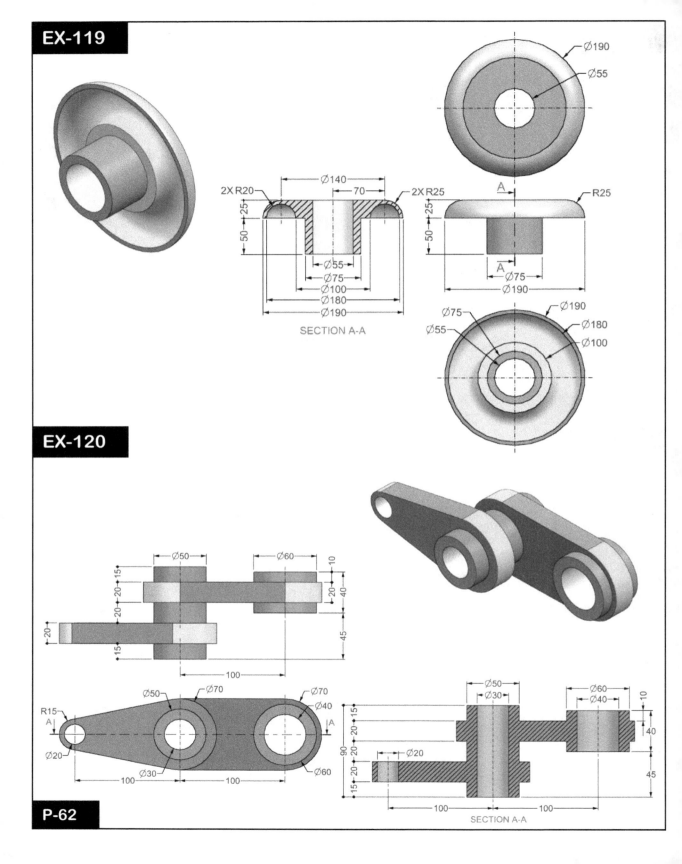

EX-119

2X R20   Ø140   2X R25   R25
70
25   25
50   50
Ø55
Ø75
Ø100
Ø180
Ø190   Ø75
Ø190
SECTION A-A

Ø190
Ø55

A
A
Ø75
Ø190

Ø75   Ø190
Ø55   Ø180
Ø100

EX-120

Ø50   Ø60   10
15   20
20   20
40
20   20
15   45
100

Ø50   Ø70   Ø70
R15   Ø40
A   A
Ø20
Ø30   Ø60
100   100

Ø50   Ø60   10
Ø30   Ø40
15   40
20
20
Ø20
15   45
100   100
SECTION A-A

P-62

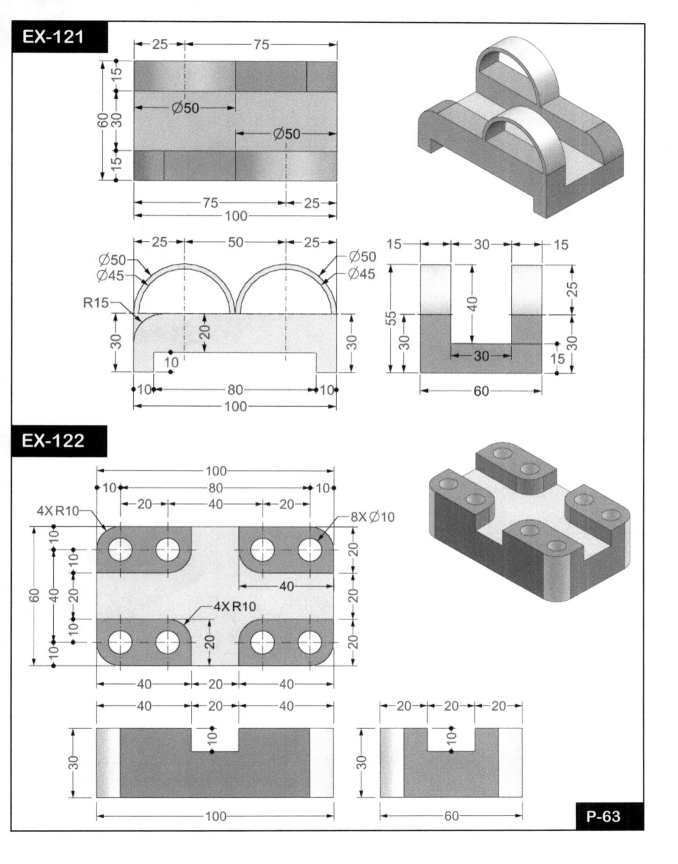

EX-121

EX-122

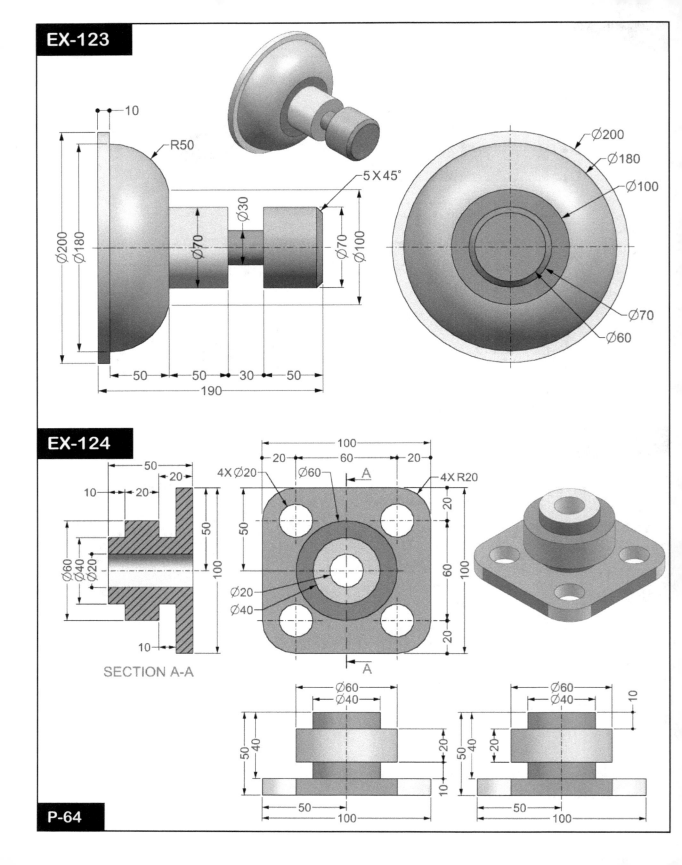

EX-123

10

R50

Ø200
Ø180

Ø30
Ø70

5 X 45°

Ø70
Ø100

Ø200
Ø180
Ø100

Ø70
Ø60

50 — 50 — 30 — 50
190

EX-124

50
10 — 20
20

4X Ø20
Ø60
A
4X R20

100
20 — 60 — 20

20

Ø60
Ø40
Ø20

50

60

100

Ø20
Ø40

20

10

SECTION A-A

A

Ø60
Ø40

50
40

50
40

20

20

Ø60
Ø40

10

50
100

50
100

P-64

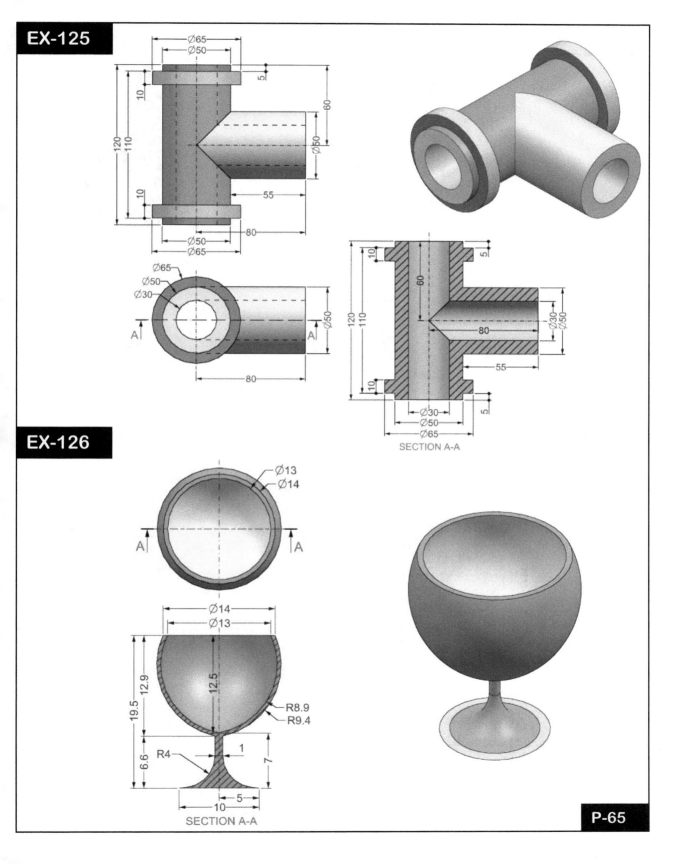

EX-125

Ø65
Ø50
5
10
120
110
60
Ø50
10
55
80
Ø50
Ø65

Ø65
Ø50
Ø30
A
A
Ø50
80

10
60
120
110
10
Ø30
Ø50
80
Ø30
Ø50
55
5
Ø30
Ø50
Ø65
SECTION A-A

EX-126

Ø13
Ø14
A
A

Ø14
Ø13
19.5
12.9
12.5
R8.9
R9.4
6.6
R4
1
7
10
5
SECTION A-A

P-65

PCD ⌀75
⌀100
8X ⌀12 THRU
ON PCD 75
⌀50
⌀30
⌀40
A | A

⌀40
⌀30
20
40
75
10
15
⌀50
75
⌀100
SECTION A-A

2X R15
2X R5
15
20
15
10.9
24.5
15
35.4

⌀50
⌀46
25.9
3
10
6
2
35.4
50.4

EX-129

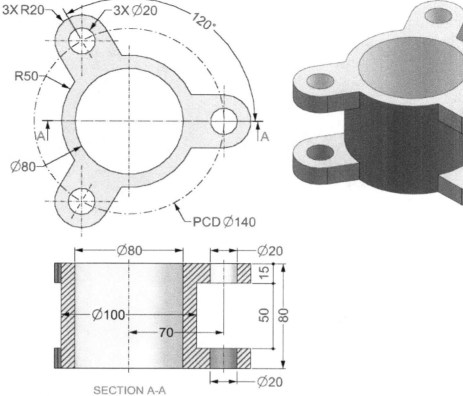

3X R20
3X Ø20
120°
R50
A
A
Ø80
PCD Ø140

Ø80
Ø20
15
Ø100
50
80
70
Ø20

SECTION A-A

EX-130

PCD Ø55
Ø70
A
A
8X Ø8
ON PCD 55
Ø30
Ø40

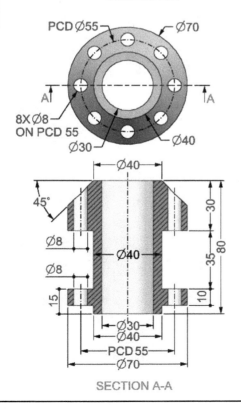

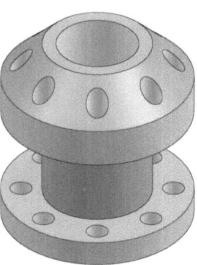

Ø40
45°
30
Ø8
Ø40
80
Ø8
35
15
10
Ø30
Ø40
PCD 55
Ø70

SECTION A-A

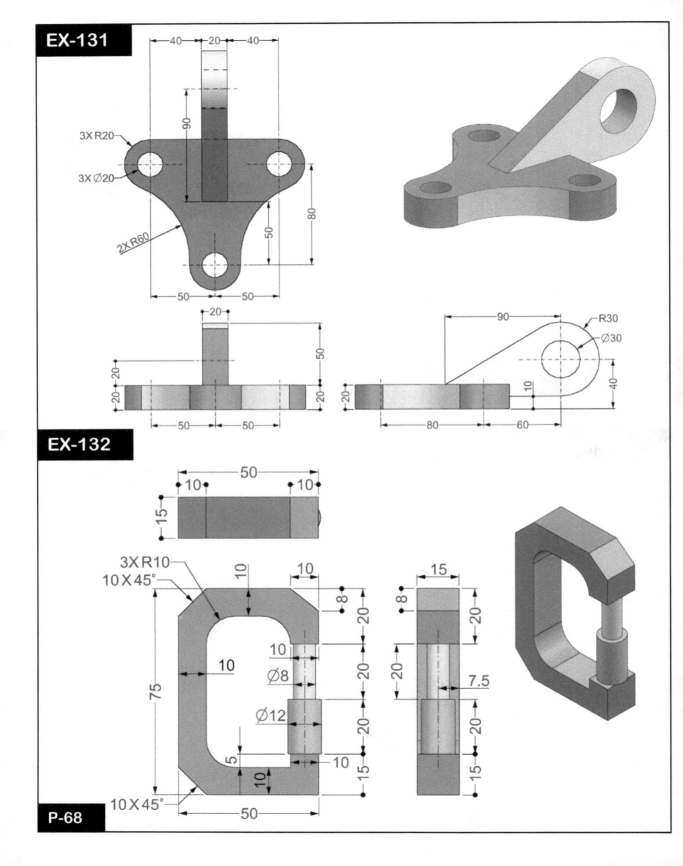

EX-131

3X R20
3X Ø20
2X R60
40 20 40
90
80
50
50 50

20
20 20
20
50 50
50

90
R30
Ø30
20
10
40
80 60

EX-132

50
10 10
15

3X R10
10 X 45°
10
10
8
20
10
Ø8
20
75
Ø12
20
5
10
10
10
50
10 X 45°

15
8
20
20
7.5
20
15

P-68

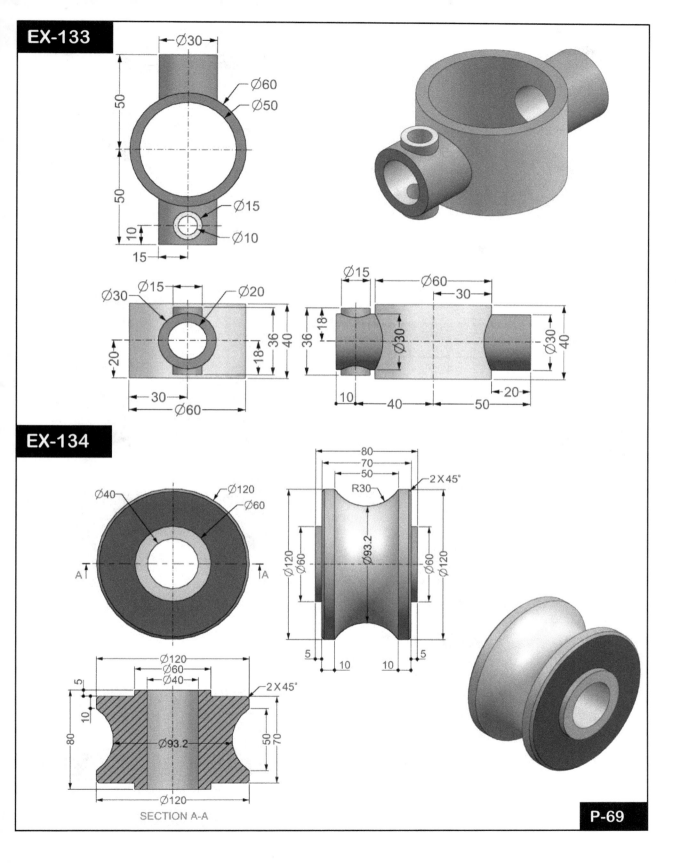

EX-133

EX-134

SECTION A-A

P-69

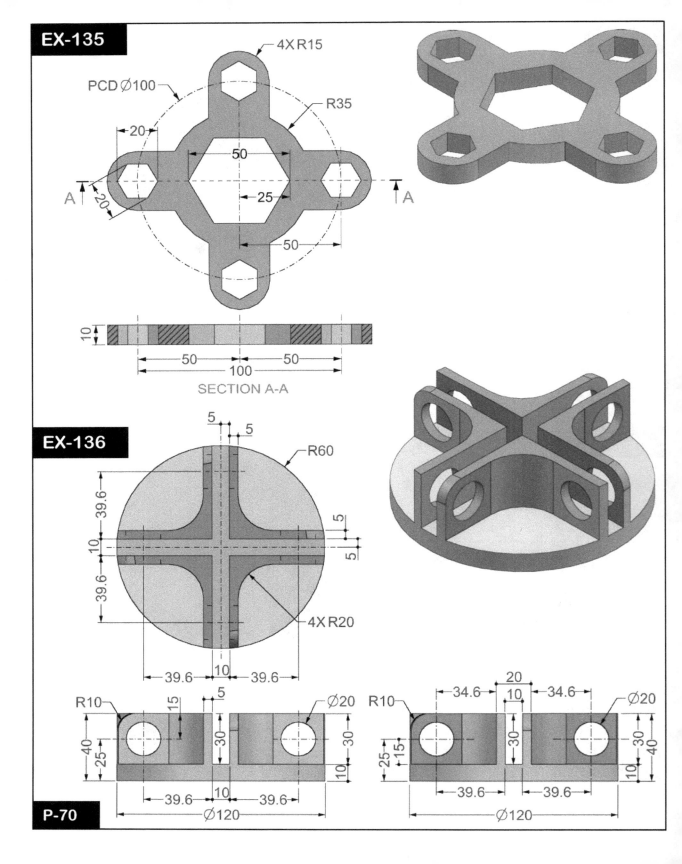

EX-135

4X R15
PCD Ø100
R35
20
50
25
50
20
A
A

10
50   50
100
SECTION A-A

EX-136

5
5
R60
39.6
5
10
5
39.6
4X R20
39.6   10   39.6

R10
15
5
Ø20
40
25
30
30
10
39.6   10   39.6
Ø120

R10
20
10
34.6   34.6
Ø20
25
15
30
30
10
40
39.6   39.6
Ø120

P-70

EX-137

2X R6
2X R5
20
10
10
15
5
10
10
34.6
10.2
10
20
10

A
A

6
B
55
3

SECTION A-A
(SCALE 1:1)

R1
1
1
1

DETAIL B
(SCALE 2:1)

SHELL THICKNESS = 1MM
ALL INSIDE WALL THICKNESS

EX-138

60°
60°
R46
R41
R50
R37
60°
9
60°
Ø12
Ø12
Ø12
60°

10
Ø12
20

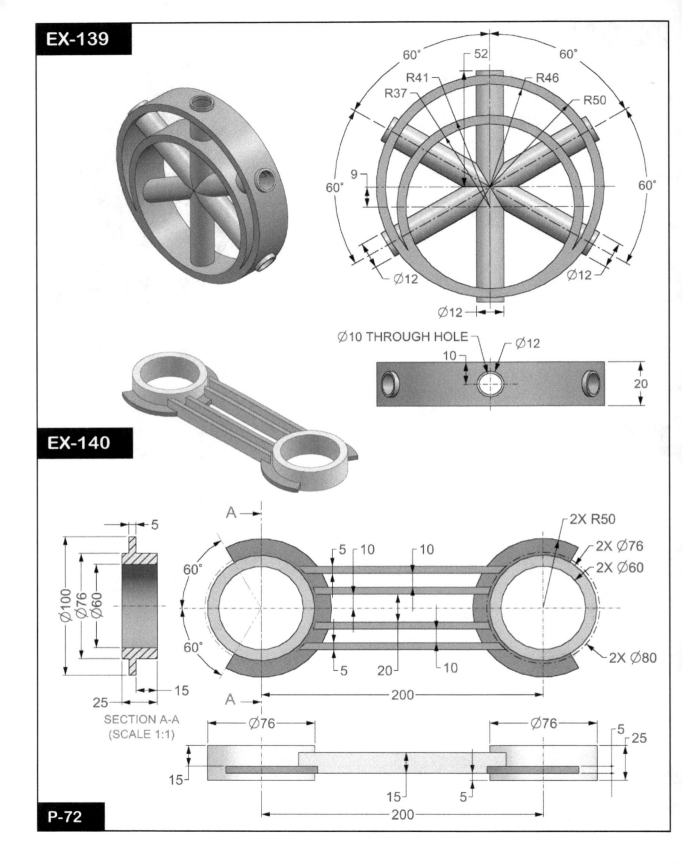

EX-139

60° 52 60°
R41 R46
R37 R50
60° 9 60°
Ø12 Ø12
Ø12

Ø10 THROUGH HOLE Ø12
10
20

EX-140

5 2X R50
2X Ø76
60° 5 10 10 2X Ø60
Ø100 Ø76 Ø60
60° 2X Ø80
5 20 10
25 15 200
SECTION A-A
(SCALE 1:1)

A

Ø76 Ø76
5 25
15 15 5
200

P-72

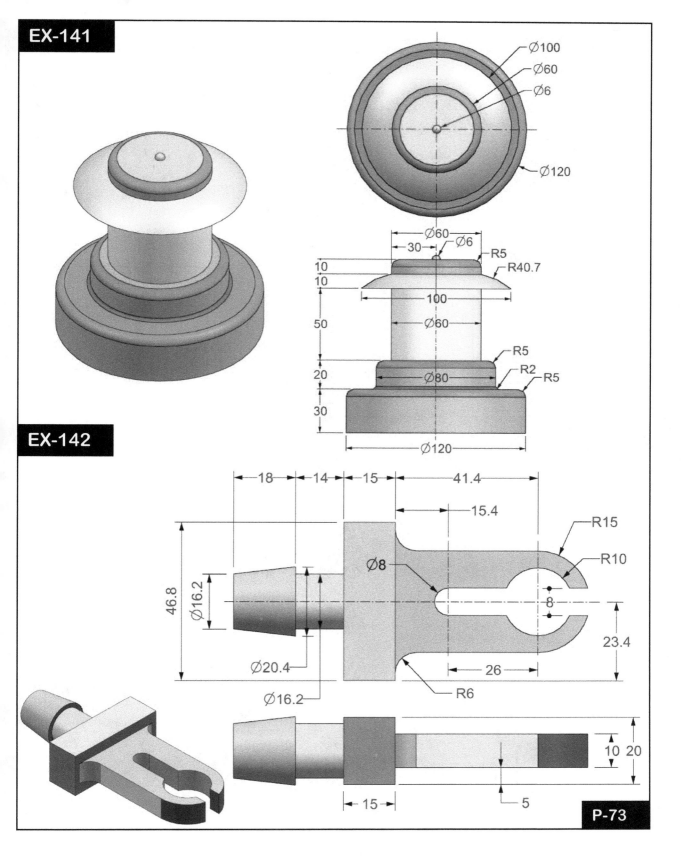

EX-141

Ø100
Ø60
Ø6
Ø120

Ø60
30
Ø6
R5
10
10
R40.7
100
50
Ø60
R5
20
Ø80
R2
R5
30
Ø120

EX-142

18
14
15
41.4

15.4

R15
R10

46.8
Ø16.2
Ø8
8
Ø20.4
23.4
Ø16.2
26
R6

10 20
15
5

P-73

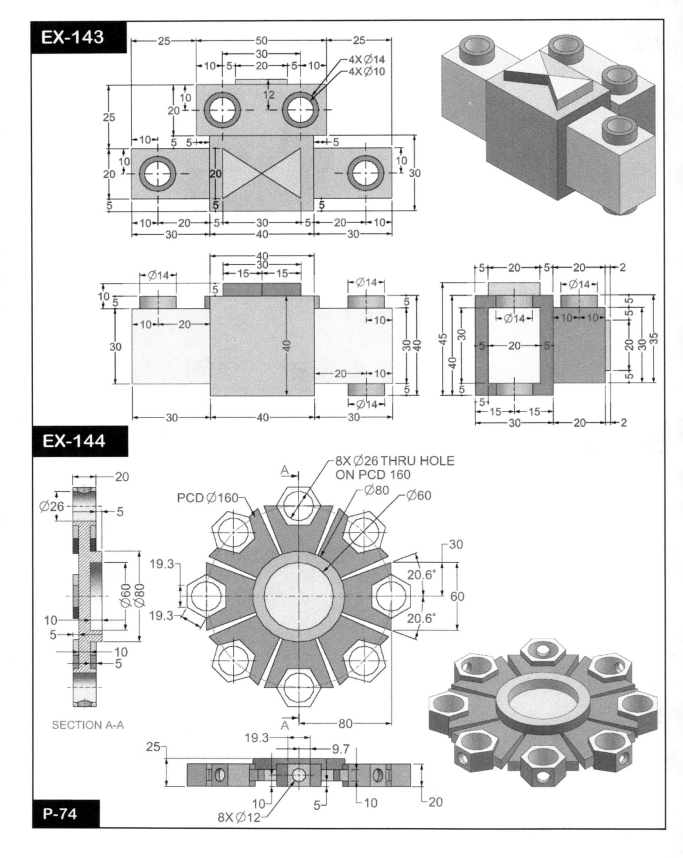

EX-143

EX-144

SECTION A-A

8X Ø26 THRU HOLE
ON PCD 160

PCD Ø160

Ø80

Ø60

8X Ø12

P-74

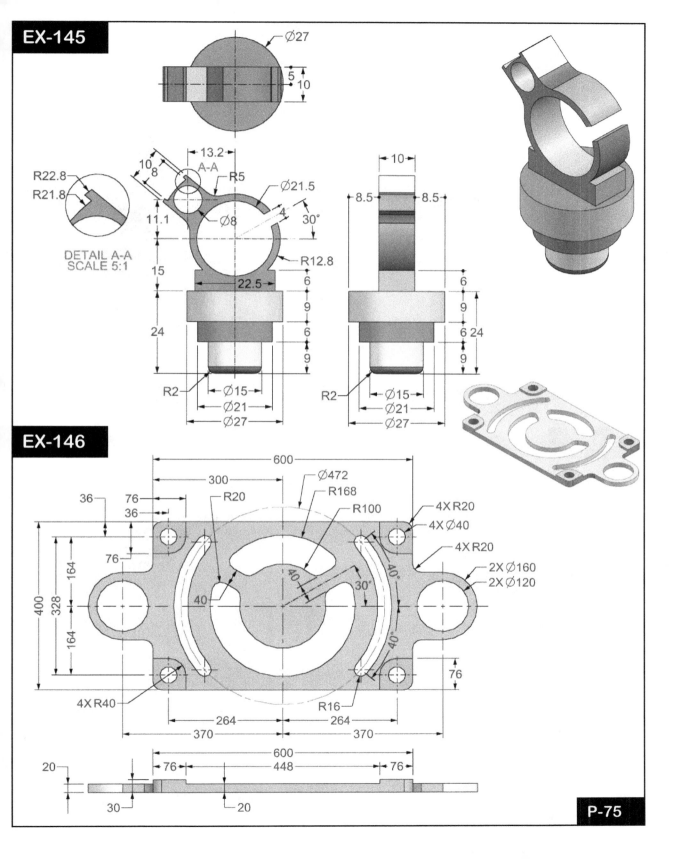

EX-145

Ø27

5
10

R22.8
R21.8

13.2
10
8
A-A
R5
Ø21.5
Ø8
4
30°
11.1
R12.8

DETAIL A-A
SCALE 5:1

15
22.5
6
9
6
9

24

R2
Ø15
Ø21
Ø27

10

8.5
8.5

6
9
6 24
9

R2
Ø15
Ø21
Ø27

EX-146

600
300
Ø472
R168
R100
R20
4X R20
4X Ø40
4X R20
2X Ø160
2X Ø120

36
76
36
76

164
328
400
164

40
40
30°
40°
40

40°

R16

76

4X R40
264
264
370
370

600
448
76
76

20
76
30
20

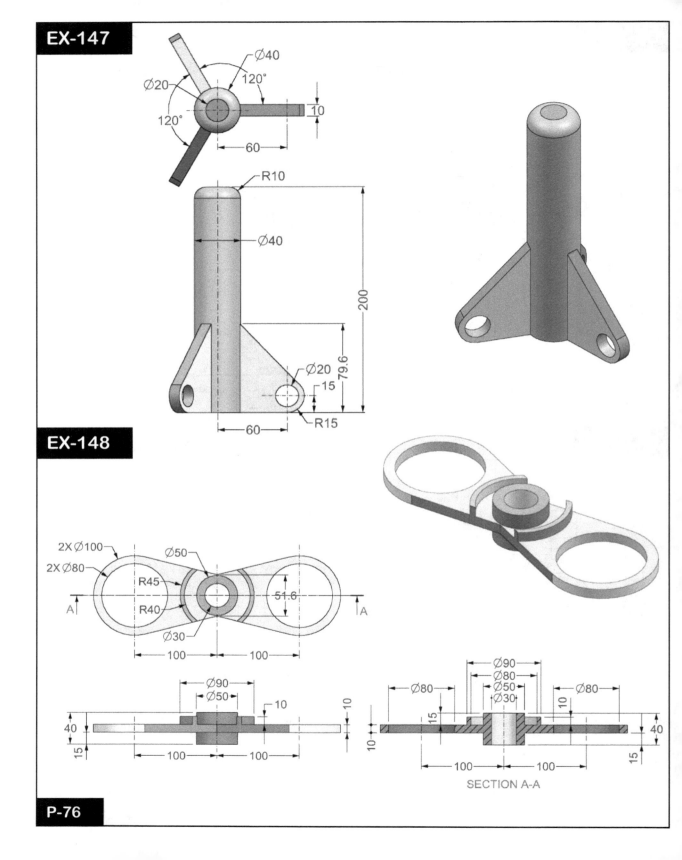

EX-147

Ø40
120°
Ø20
120°
10
60

R10
Ø40
200
79.6
Ø20
15
60
R15

EX-148

2X Ø100
2X Ø80
Ø50
R45
51.6
A
R40
A
Ø30
100
100

Ø90
Ø50
10
10
40
15
100
100

Ø90
Ø80
Ø50
Ø30
Ø80
Ø80
10
15
40
10
15
100
100
SECTION A-A

P-76

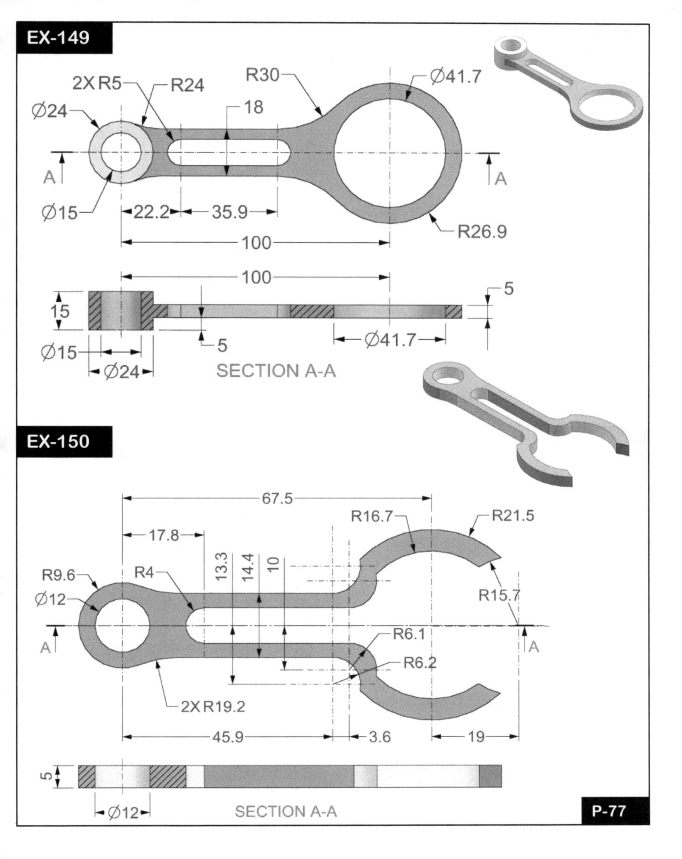

EX-149

2X R5 — R24

R30

Ø41.7

Ø24

18

R26.9

A

A

Ø15

22.2 — 35.9

100

100

15

5

Ø15

Ø24

5

Ø41.7

SECTION A-A

EX-150

67.5

R16.7

R21.5

17.8

13.3 14.4 10

R9.6

R4

R15.7

Ø12

R6.1

A

A

R6.2

2X R19.2

45.9

3.6

19

5

Ø12

SECTION A-A

P-77

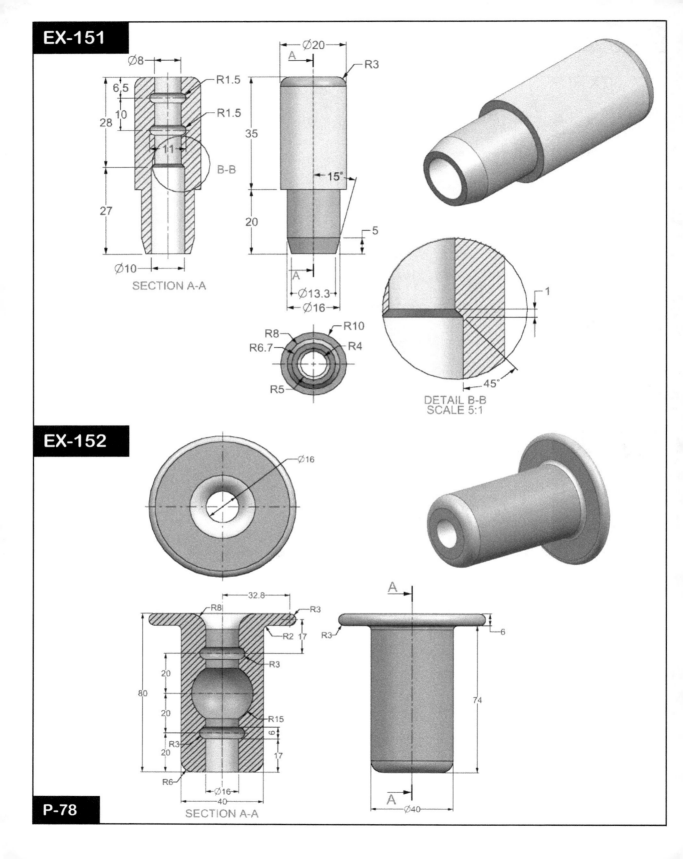

EX-151

SECTION A-A

DETAIL B-B
SCALE 5:1

EX-152

SECTION A-A

P-78

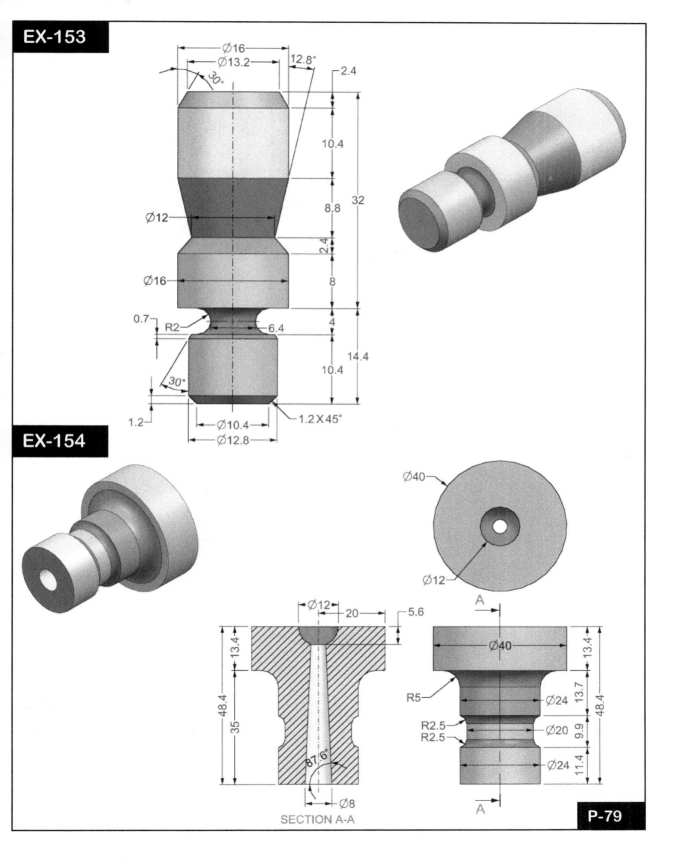

EX-153

EX-154

SECTION A-A

P-79

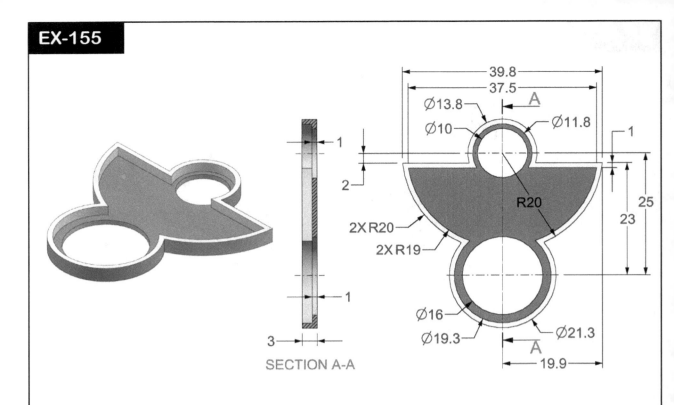

SECTION A-A

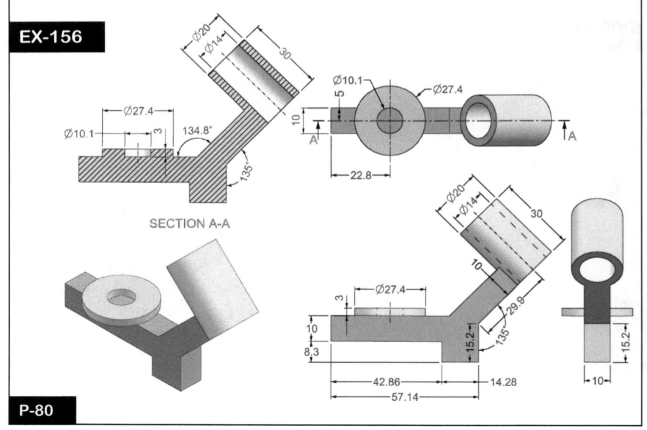

SECTION A-A

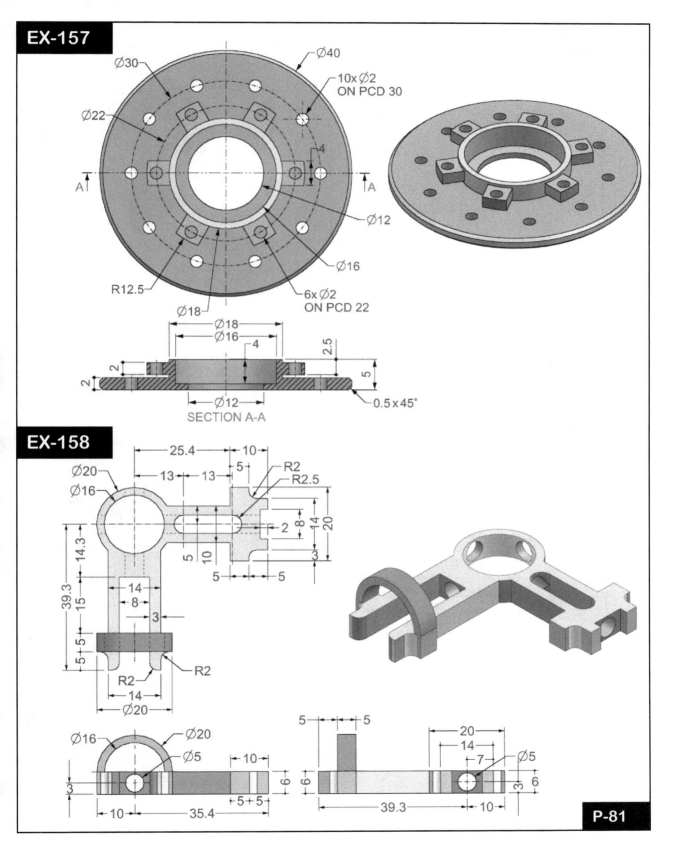

EX-157

Ø30
Ø40
10x Ø2
ON PCD 30
Ø22
4
A
A
Ø12
Ø16
R12.5
6x Ø2
ON PCD 22
Ø18

Ø18
Ø16
4
2.5
2
5
2
Ø12
0.5 x 45°
SECTION A-A

EX-158

25.4
10
13
13
5
R2
R2.5
Ø20
Ø16
2
8
14
20
14.3
5
10
3
39.3
5
14
8
3
15
5
5
R2
14
R2
Ø20

Ø16
Ø20
Ø5
10
3
6
5 5
10
35.4

5
5
20
14
7
Ø5
6
6
3
39.3
10

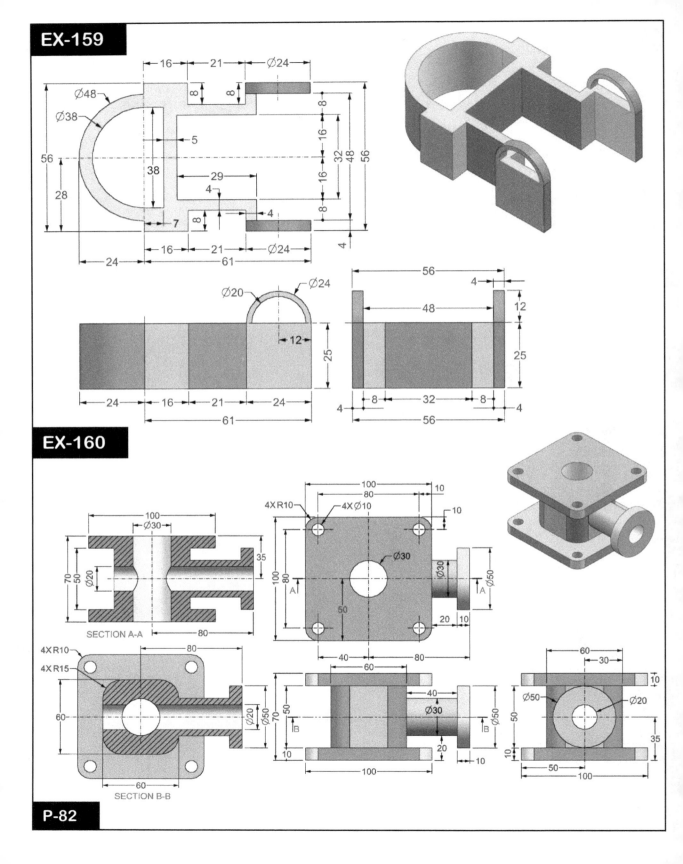

EX-159

EX-160

SECTION A-A

SECTION B-B

P-82

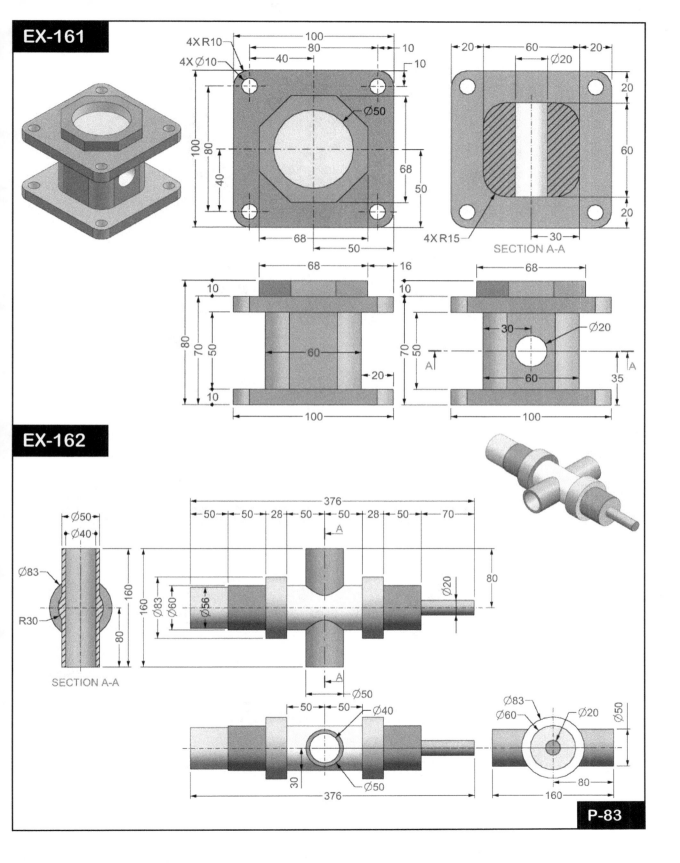

EX-161

4X R10
4X Ø10
100
80
40
10
10
Ø50
100
80
40
68
50
68
50

20
60
Ø20
20
20
60
20
4X R15
30
SECTION A-A

68
16
10
10
80
70
50
60
20
10
100

68
10
30
Ø20
70
50
A
60
A
35
100

EX-162

376
50
50
28
50
50
28
50
70
A

Ø50
Ø40
Ø83
160
R30
160
Ø83
Ø60
Ø56
80
Ø20
80
SECTION A-A
A

Ø50
50
50
Ø40
30
Ø50
376

Ø83
Ø60
Ø20
Ø50
80
160

P-83

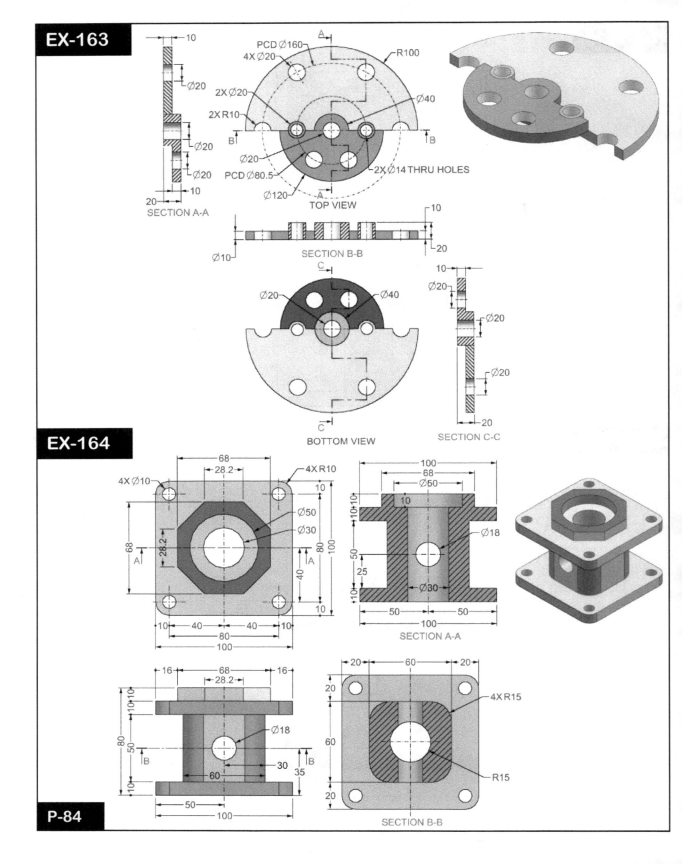

EX-163

10
Ø20
Ø20
Ø20
20 10
SECTION A-A

A
PCD Ø160
4X Ø20
R100
2X Ø20
2X R10
Ø40
B
B
Ø20
2X Ø14 THRU HOLES
PCD Ø80.5
Ø120
A
TOP VIEW

10
20
SECTION B-B
Ø10

C
Ø20
Ø40
Ø20
C
BOTTOM VIEW

10
Ø20
Ø20
Ø20
20
SECTION C-C

EX-164

68
28.2
4X Ø10
4X R10
10
Ø50
Ø30
80
68
28.2
A
A
100
40
10
10 40 40 10
80
100

100
68
Ø50
10
10+10
Ø18
50
25
10+10
Ø30
50 50
100
SECTION A-A

16 68 16
28.2
10+10
80
50
Ø18
B
B
30
60
35
10
50
100

20 60 20
20
4X R15
60
20
R15
SECTION B-B

P-84

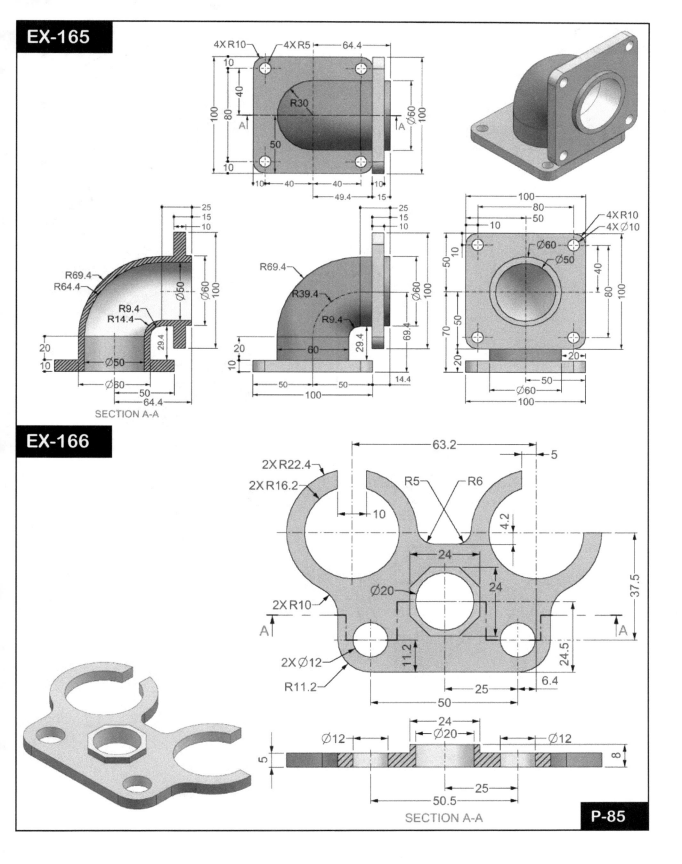

EX-165

4X R10   4X R5   64.4
10
40
80
100
R30
Ø60
100
A| |A
50
10
10   40   40   10
49.4   15

25
15
10
R69.4
R64.4
Ø50
Ø60
100
R9.4
R14.4
29.4
Ø50
20
10
Ø60
50
64.4
SECTION A-A

25
15
10
R69.4
R39.4
Ø60
100
R9.4
69.4
29.4
20
10
60
14.4
50   50
100

100
80
50
10
4X R10
4X Ø10
Ø60
Ø50
50
10
40
80
100
50
70
20
20
50
Ø60
100

EX-166

63.2   5
2X R22.4
2X R16.2
R5   R6
10
4.2
24
Ø20
24
2X R10
A| |A
11.2
2X Ø12
24.5
R11.2
6.4
25
50

24
Ø12   Ø20   Ø12
5
8
24
25
50.5
SECTION A-A

P-85

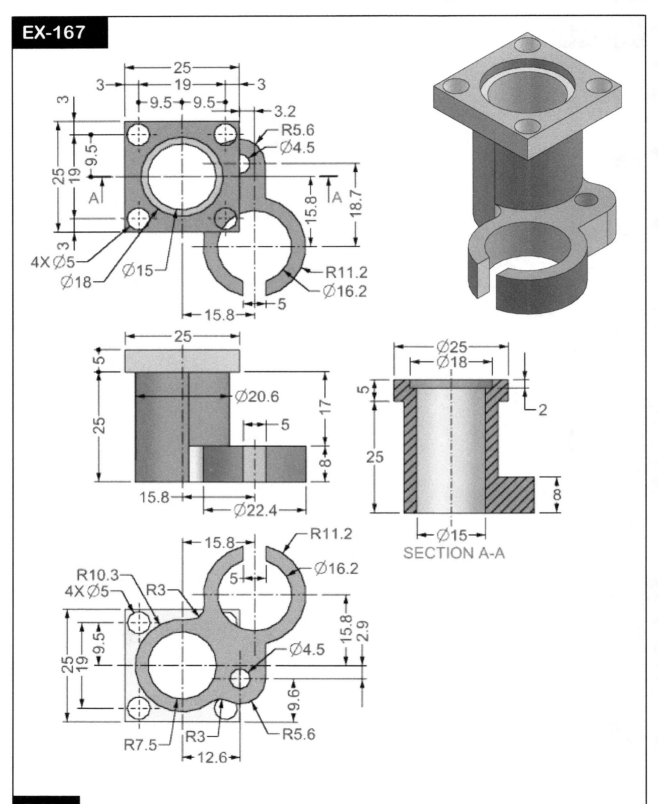

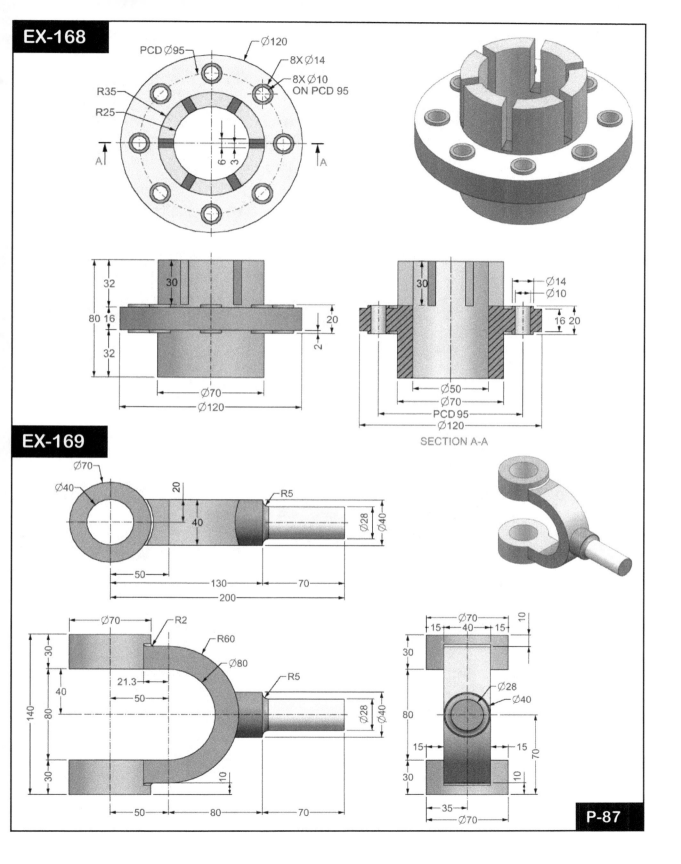

EX-168

PCD Ø95
Ø120
8X Ø14
8X Ø10
ON PCD 95
R35
R25
6 3
A A

32
30
80 16
20
32
2
Ø70
Ø120

30
Ø14
Ø10
16 20
Ø50
Ø70
PCD 95
Ø120
SECTION A-A

EX-169

Ø70
Ø40
20
40
R5
Ø28
Ø40
50
130
70
200

Ø70
R2
R60
Ø80
R5
30
21.3
50
40
80
140
80
Ø28
Ø40
30
10
50
80
70

Ø70
15 40 15
10
30
30
80
Ø28
Ø40
15
15
70
30
10
35
Ø70

P-87

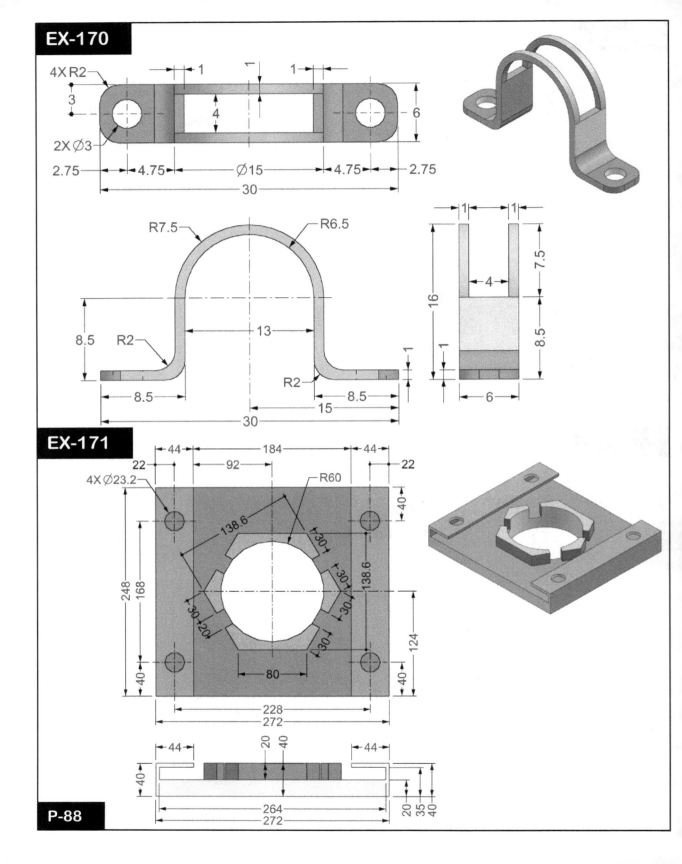

EX-170

4X R2
3
2X Ø3
2.75
4.75
Ø15
4.75
2.75
30
1
1
4
6

R7.5
R6.5
R2
8.5
13
R2
8.5
8.5
15
30

1
1
7.5
4
16
1
8.5
6

EX-171

44
184
44
22
92
22
4X Ø23.2
R60
138.6
30
30
40
248
168
138.6
30
30
30
20
30
124
80
40
228
272

44
20
40
44
40
40
264
272
20
35
40

P-88

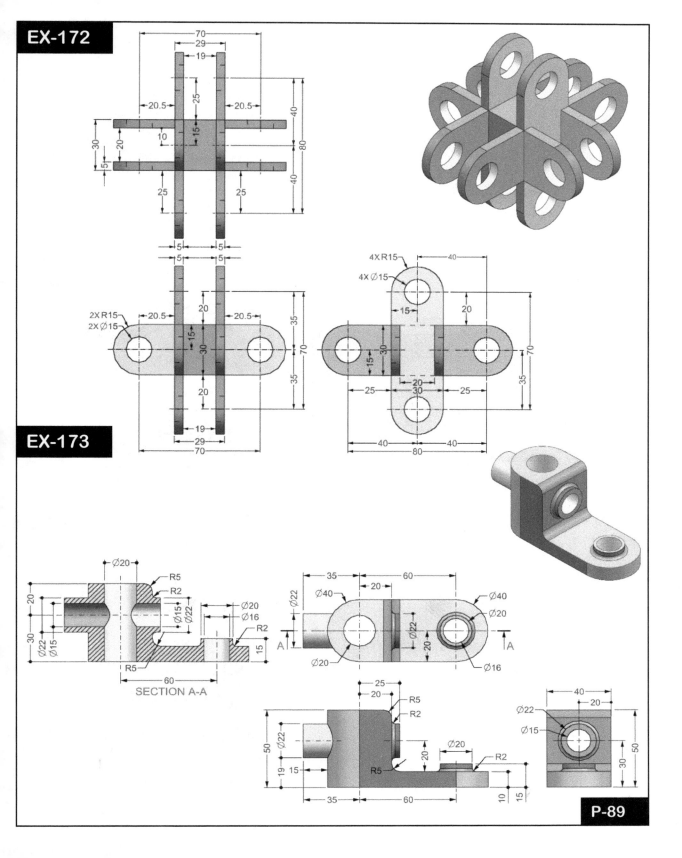

EX-172

EX-173

SECTION A-A

P-89

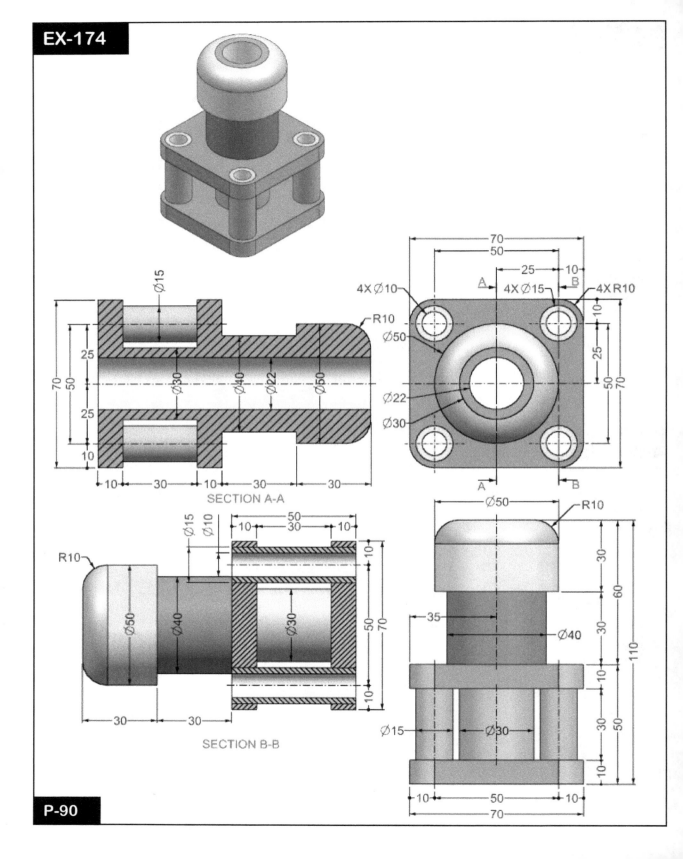

EX-174

SECTION A-A

SECTION B-B

P-90

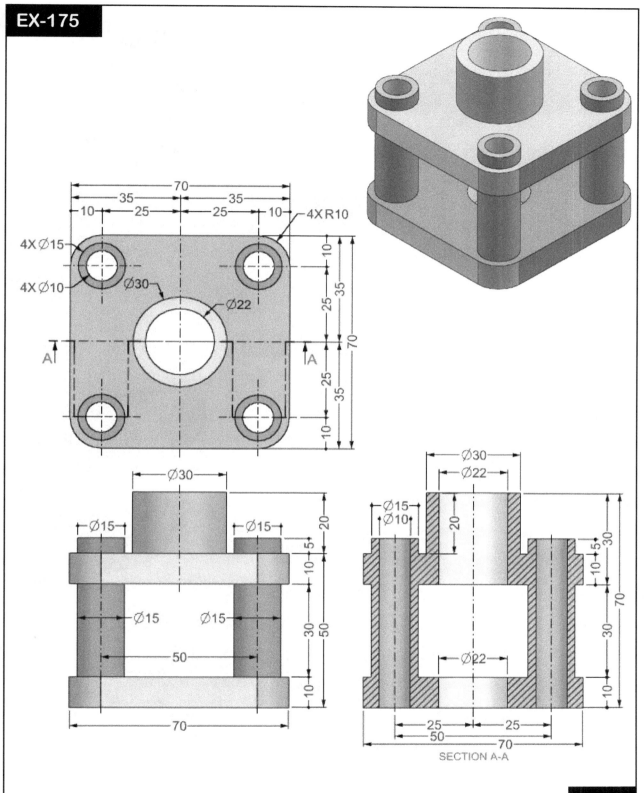

EX-175

4X⌀15
4X⌀10
⌀30
⌀22
4X R10

70
35
35
10
25
25
10
10
25
35
70
25
35
10

A
A

⌀30
⌀15
⌀15
⌀15
⌀15
50
70
20
5
10
30
50
10

⌀30
⌀22
⌀15
⌀10
⌀22
20
30
5
10
30
70
10
25
25
50
70

SECTION A-A

P-91

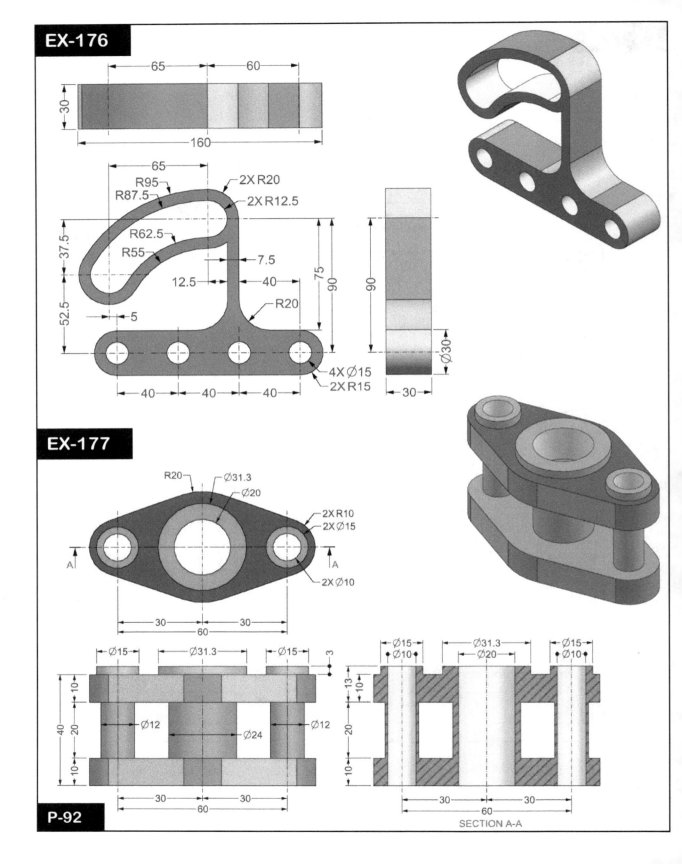

EX-176

EX-177

P-92

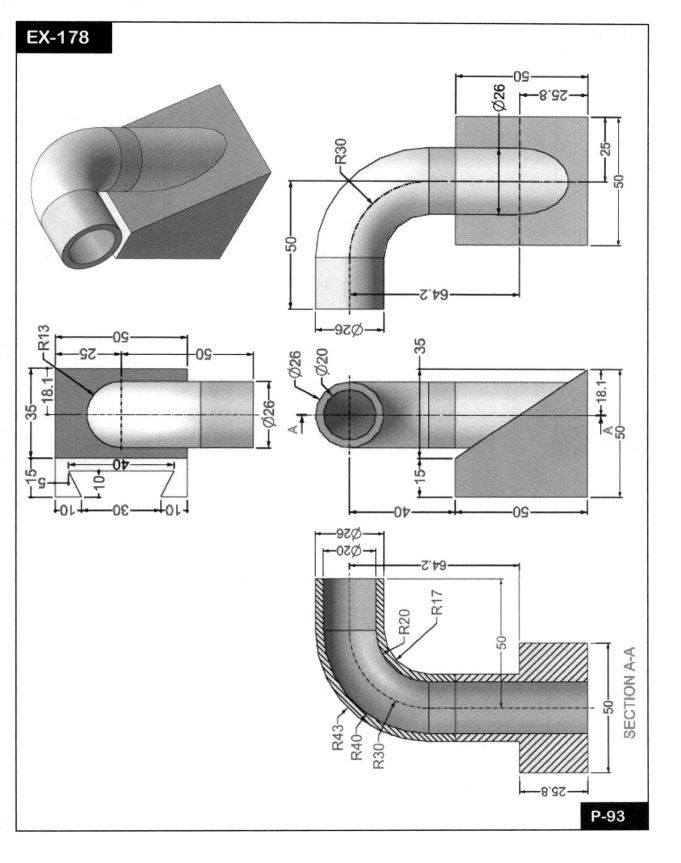

EX-178

Ø26
Ø20
Ø26

50
25.8
Ø26
R30
25
50
64.2

R13
50
25
50
18.1
35
Ø26
15
5
40
10
10
30
10

Ø26
Ø20
A
35
18.1
A
50
15
40
50

Ø26
Ø20
64.2
R20
R17
50
R43
R40
R30
50
25.8

SECTION A-A

P-93

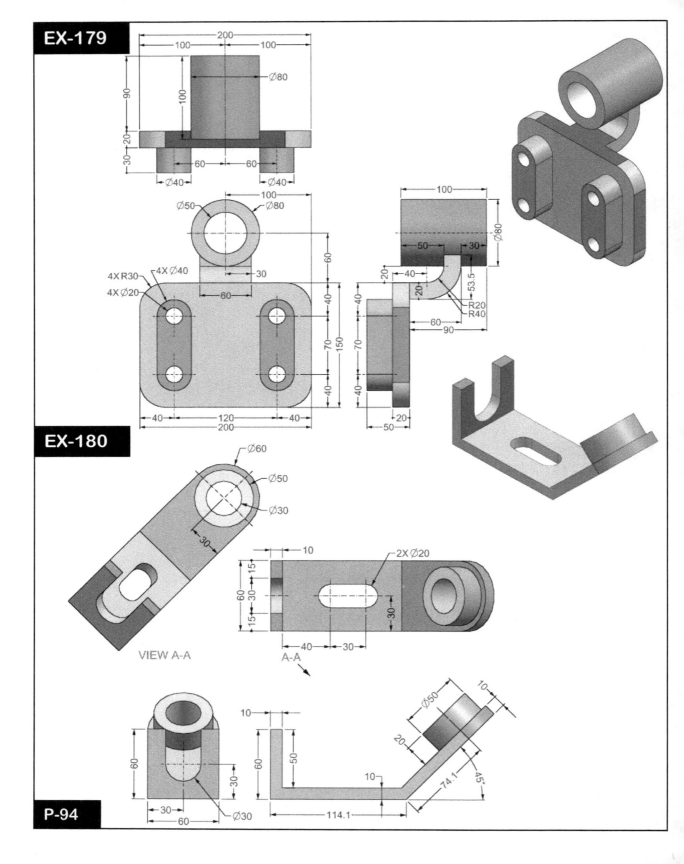

EX-179

EX-180

VIEW A-A

A-A

P-94

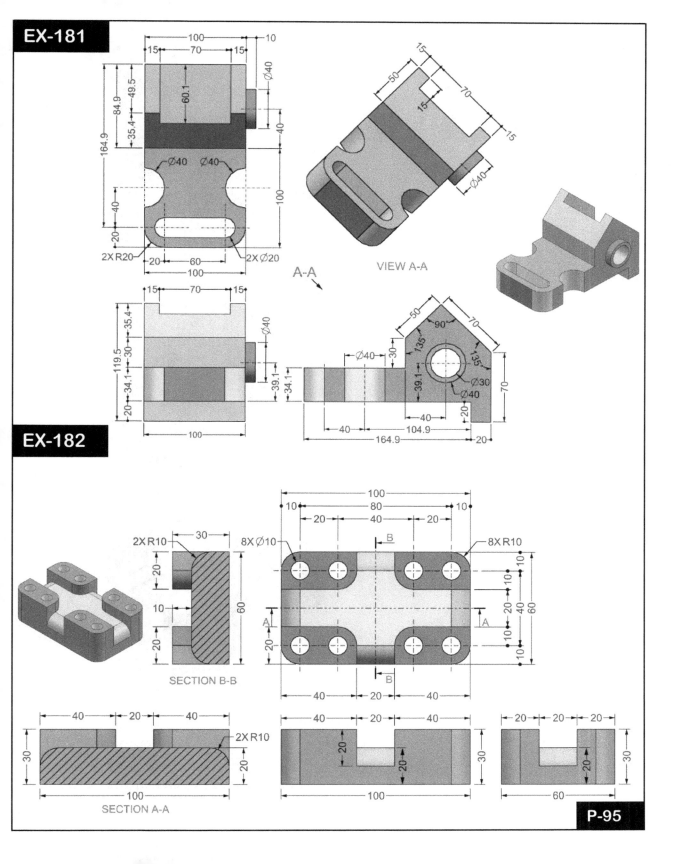

EX-181

VIEW A-A

A-A

EX-182

2X R10

30

8X Ø10

8X R10

B

SECTION B-B

A

A

B

2X R10

SECTION A-A

P-95

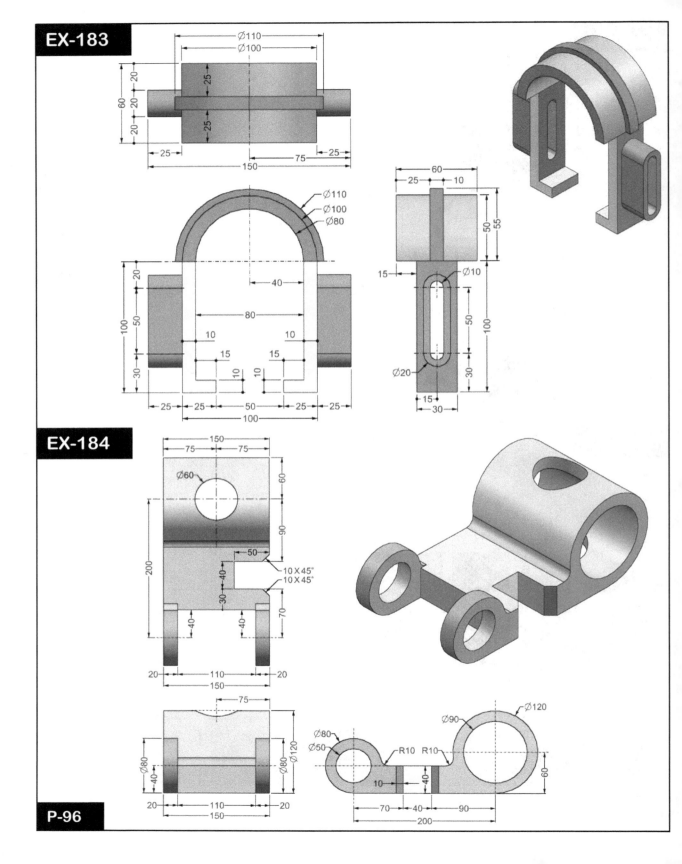

EX-183

EX-184

P-96

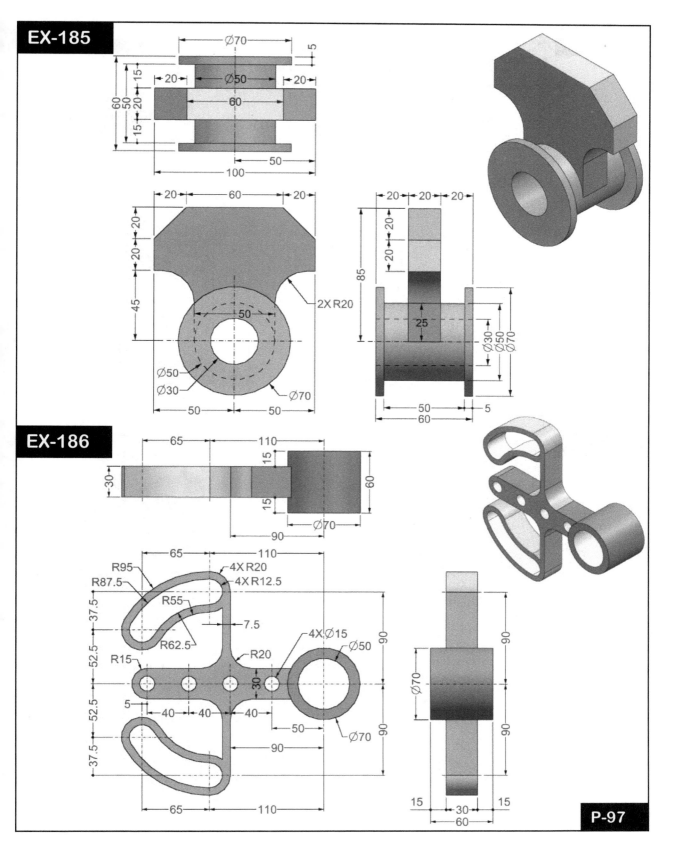

EX-185

EX-186

P-97

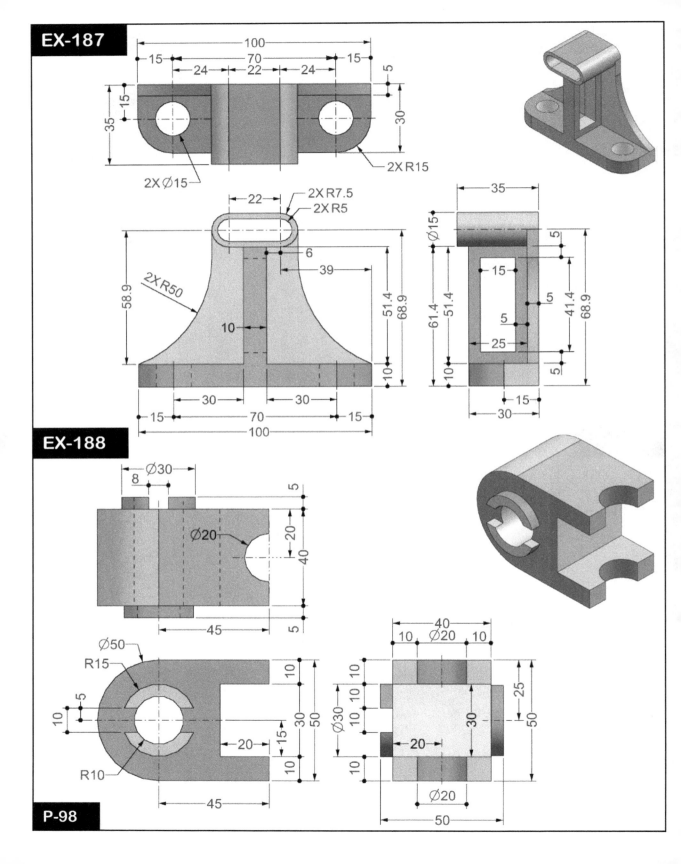

EX-187

2X Ø15
2X R15
2X R7.5
2X R5
2X R50

EX-188

Ø30
Ø20
Ø50
R15
R10

P-98

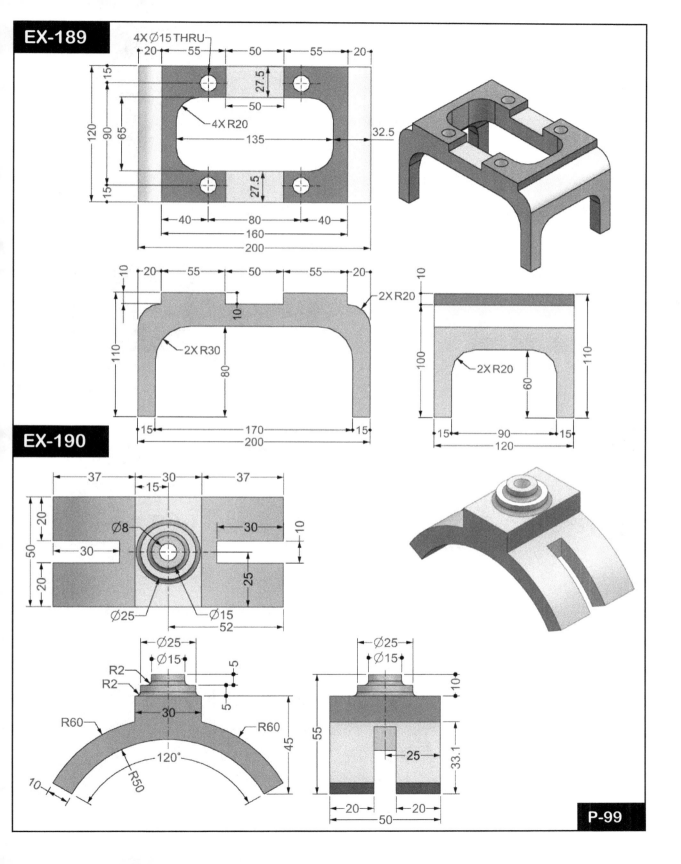

EX-189

EX-190

P-99

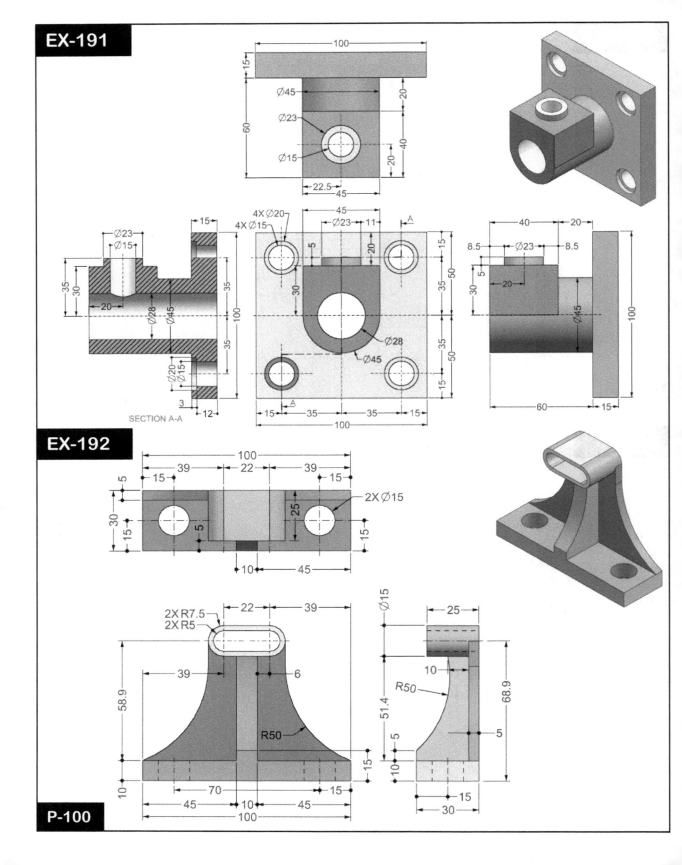

EX-191

SECTION A-A

EX-192

P-100

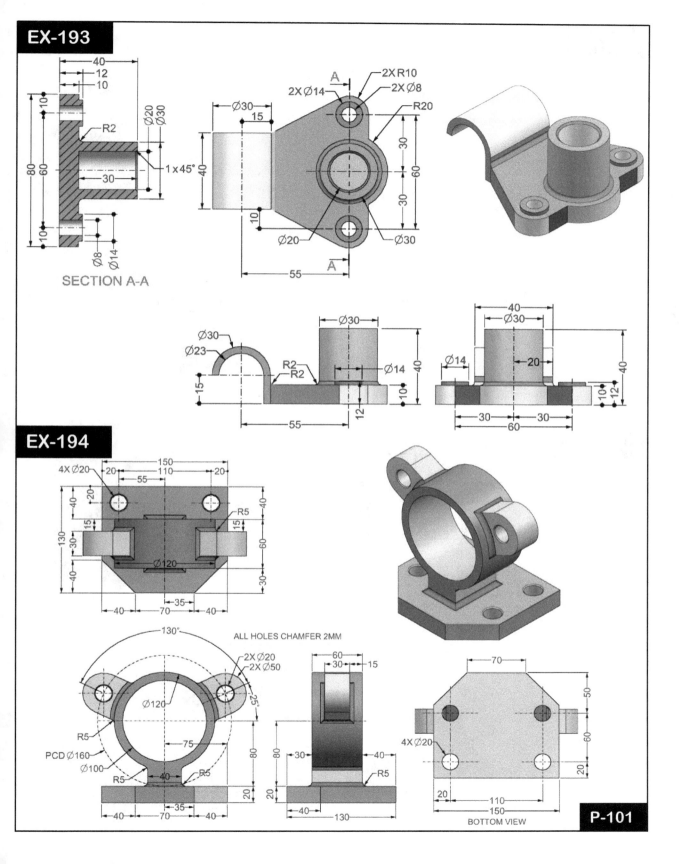

EX-193

SECTION A-A

2X R10
2X Ø14
2X Ø8
R20
Ø30
15
Ø20
Ø30
40
10
55
Ø30
Ø23
R2
R2
Ø14
15
10
12
55
40
Ø30
Ø14
20
40
10
12
30
30
60

EX-194

150
4X Ø20
20
110
20
55
20
40
40
15
130
R5
30
15
60
Ø120
40
30
40
35
40
70

ALL HOLES CHAMFER 2MM

130°
2X Ø20
2X Ø50
25°
Ø120
R5
75
PCD Ø160
Ø100
80
R5
R5
40
20
40
70
40
35

60
30
15
80
30
40
80
R5
20
40
130
R5

70
50
60
4X Ø20
20
20
110
150

BOTTOM VIEW

P-101

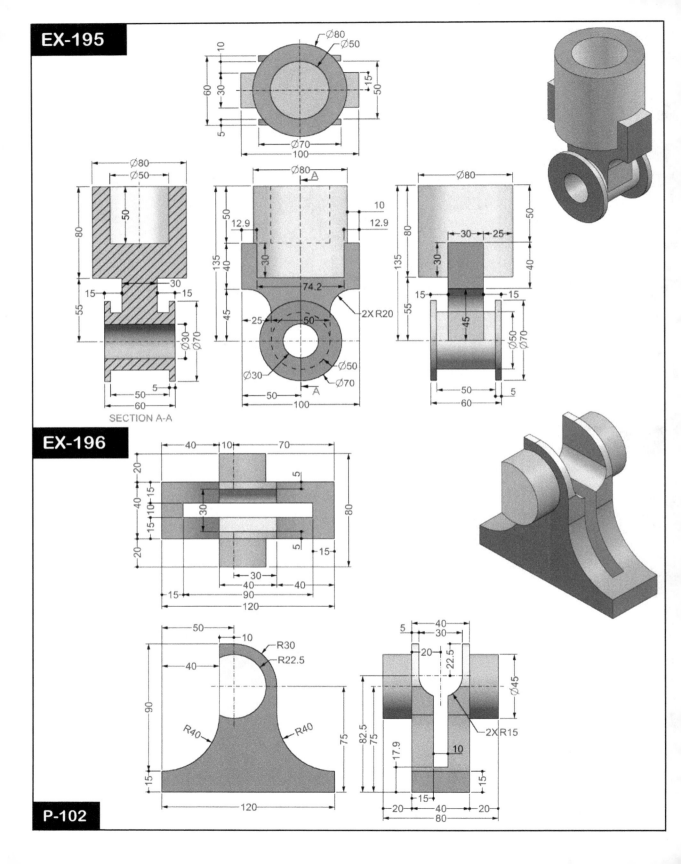

EX-195

∅80
∅50
10
60
30
15
50
5
∅70
100

∅80
∅50
80
50
15
15
30
∅30
∅70
50
5
60
SECTION A-A

∅80
A
50
135
12.9
30
74.2
40
45
25
50
2X R20
∅30
∅50
∅70
50
100
A
10
12.9

∅80
80
135
30
30
25
55
15
15
45
∅50
∅70
50
5
60

EX-196

40
10
70
20
40
15
10
30
15
5
5
80
20
15
30
40
40
15
90
120

50
10
R30
R22.5
40
90
R40
R40
75
15
120

5
40
30
20
22.5
∅45
82.5
75
17.9
10
2X R15
15
15
20
40
20
80

P-102

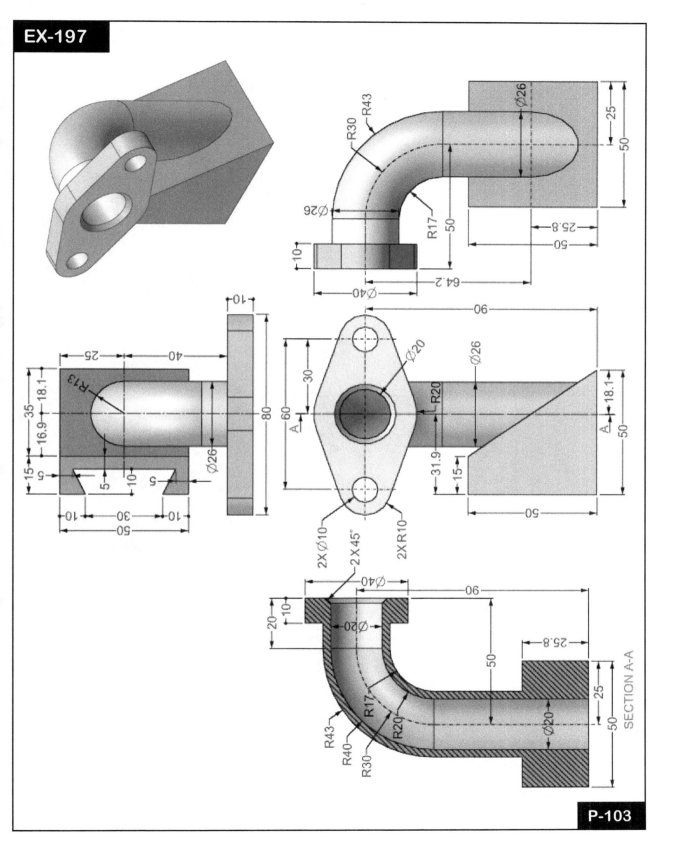

SECTION A-A

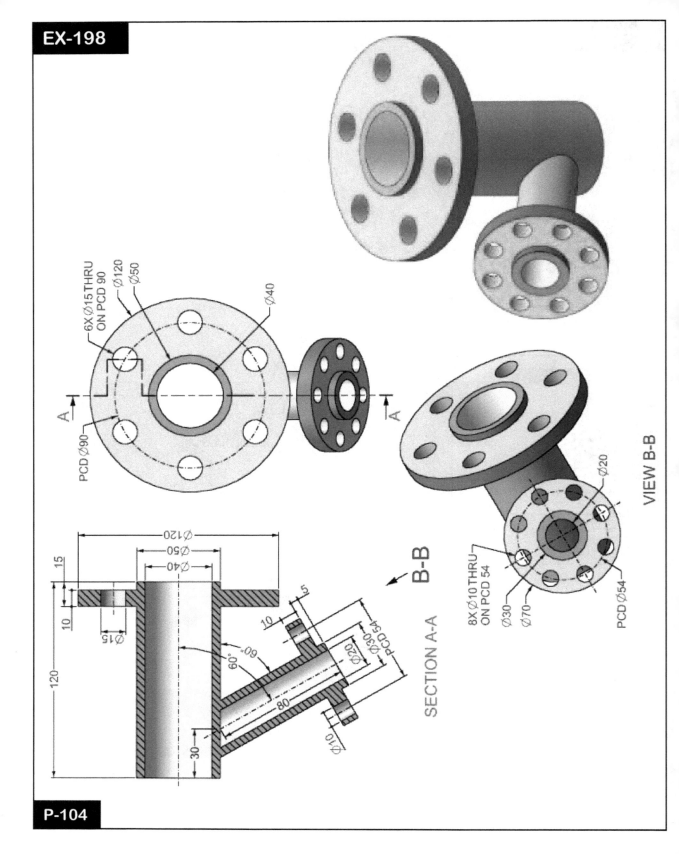

6X Ø15 THRU
ON PCD 90
Ø120
Ø50
Ø40

A

PCD Ø90

Ø120
Ø50
Ø40

15
10
Ø15

120

30

B-B

60°
60°

80

Ø10

5
10
Ø30
Ø20
PCD 54

SECTION A-A

VIEW B-B

Ø20

8X Ø10 THRU
ON PCD 54
Ø30
Ø70
PCD Ø54

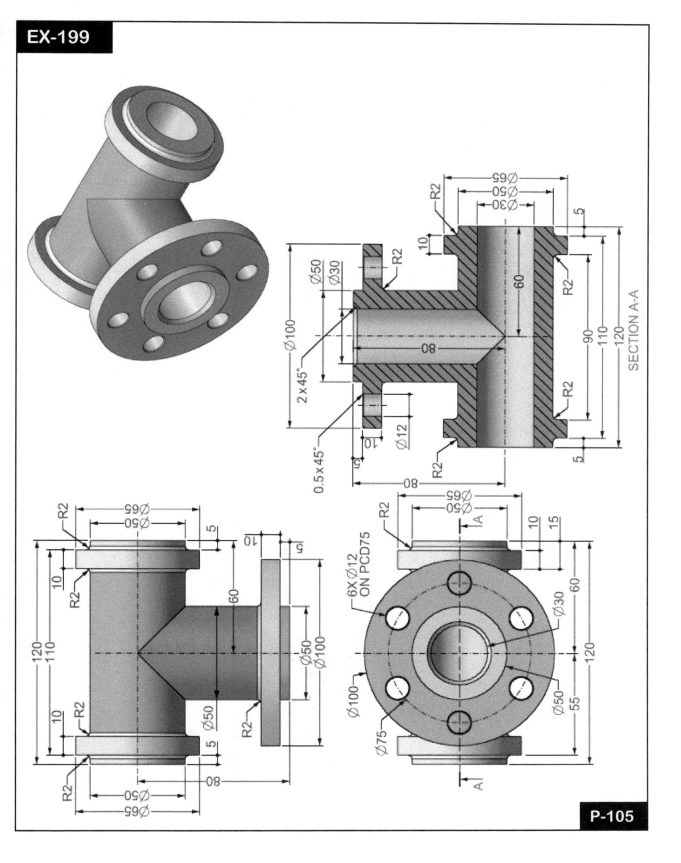

EX-199

SECTION A-A

P-105

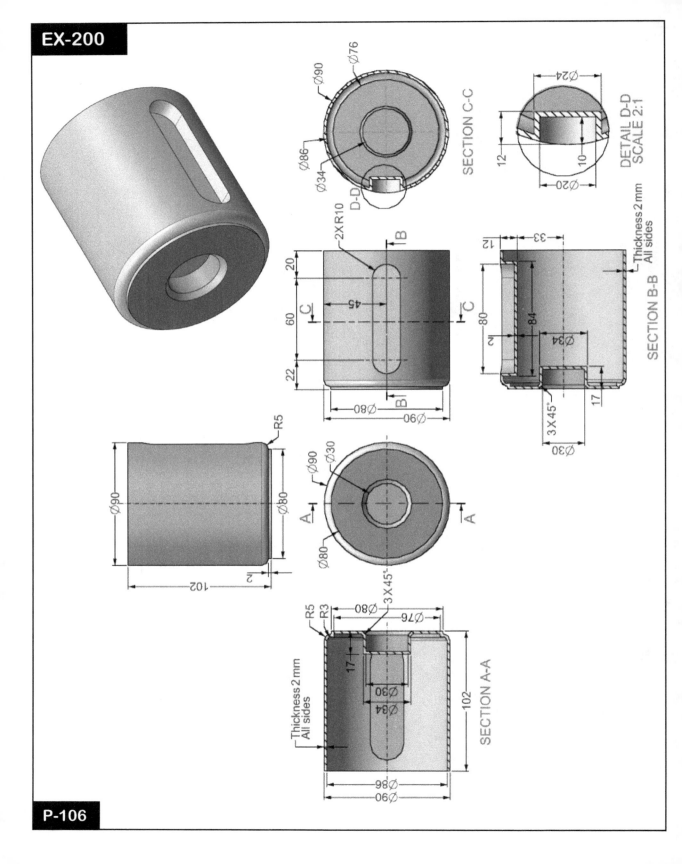

EX-200

P-106

SECTION C-C

Ø76
Ø90
Ø86
Ø34
D-D

DETAIL D-D
SCALE 2:1
Ø24
12
10
Ø20

2X R10
B
20
45
60
C
22
B
Ø80
Ø90

Thickness 2 mm
All sides
12
33
80
84
Ø34
2
3 X 45°
17
Ø30
SECTION B-B

R5
Ø90
Ø80
102
2

Ø90
Ø30
Ø80
A
A
3 X 45°

R5
R3
Ø80
Ø76
17
Ø84
Ø30
Thickness 2 mm
All sides
98Ø
Ø90
102
SECTION A-A

www.ingramcontent.com/pod-product-compliance
Lightning Source LLC
Chambersburg PA
CBHW060159060326
40690CB00018B/4172